TRIUMPH
ENTERTAINMENT

Credits:

- Editor in Chief.. Bill Gill, AKA "Pojo"
- Creative Director & Graphic Design............. Jon Anderson
- Publisher.. Bob Baker
- Contributors .... Vijay Seixas, Nick Moore, Chris Schroeder, Augustine Choy, Ken Jackson, Adam Forristal, Evan Vargas.

Want to get involved?

I've been doing collectible card game books and magazines since October 1999. I have to admit ... it's a great job! We've made close to fifty different titles during that time frame. We've been doing books more lately. I personally think books are better for the fans as you can buy them any time. They don't disappear from the newsstands in four weeks time like our magazines do.

When we were doing our monthly Pokemon Magazine, and a new set came out (like Team Rocket), you had to buy that magazine within four weeks' time and before it sold out. If you wanted to see card reviews on all the Team Rocket cards, and you were two weeks late ... you were out of luck!

And during the early years of Pokemon, our magazines sold out quite often. But with books ... you don't have that problem. You can simply order them online from places like Amazon.com, or pick one up from your local bookstore. If your local bookstore doesn't have it in stock ... get the ISBN # of the book, and have them order you one! Niceness!

But there is one thing I miss ... fan letters and fan art! I especially miss fans' fake cards. We used to show a lot of them in our monthly Pokemon Magazine. And you know what? I'd love to post them again.

So ... if you are a good artist and want to create fake Yu-Gi-Oh! cards, then by all means ... Send Them to Us! We'll display what we feel are the best dozen or so in an upcoming title. Here's an address you can contact us at:

Pojo's Books & Magazines
P.O. Box 95649
Hoffman Estates, IL 60195

Pojo

P.S. – Don't forget ... you can always stay on top of the current news, Killer Decks, Tips & Top 10 Lists by visiting our website at www.pojo.com .

Inside Pojo´s UNOFFICIAL Guide to
LEGACY OF DARKNESS

Legacy of Darkness
impact on the game

By-Augustine Choy, a.k.a. Wartortle32

Legacy of Darkness is composed of the Japanese sets Struggle of Chaos and Mythological Age. LOD's release will change the way you play your game and it will change the look of current popular decks. I'll try to review every current deck type and point out a few universal cards or strategies that make sense to use in the new environment.

However, I can't cover everything. If I don't review your type of deck, you'll have to use your head to figure out how this set can help you.

The main themes of this set are dragons, fiends, warriors, and spirits. Dragon decks haven't seen much play since the Legend of Blue Eyes set. There simply weren't enough good lower level dragons to support Dragon decks so that they could compete with other decks.

New Dragons

Now with Legacy of Darkness, Dragon decks get a few good level four dragons such as Spear Dragon and Cave Dragon. Spear Dragon is perfect for attacking face down monsters as they are usually flip effects with weak defenses. Or you can use it to take out those pesky Scapegoats, letting you do massive damage.

The only drawback is the switch to defense. In some cases, it may work to your advantage. You can attack a weaker monster and then have it protect your LP from a stronger monster.

Cave Dragon isn't nearly as good. It can be very useful when you summon it first turn and then play another dragon next turn so it can attack.

Dragon decks also got some extremely good high level dragons – namely Tyrant Dragon – which are good for clearing your opponent's field, letting you attack him or her directly with your other monsters.

A Fiendish Improvement

The same problem held true for Fiend decks. There weren't many cards you could include in a Fiend deck outside Summoned Skull, Dark Necrofear, or perhaps Giant Germ. In the new set, you receive a very good tribute monster, perhaps replacing Summoned Skull. I'm talking, of course, about Dark Ruler Ha Des. It's only 50 ATK points below Summoned Skull, but more importantly, it is 50 ATK points above the deadly Jinzo.

By only requiring one tribute and being able to negate any Effects of the monsters your Fiend monsters destroy, this card is a force to be reckoned with. Unfortunately, it probably is the only good Fiend monster that comes out of this set. The other Fiend monsters have nice Effects, but their attack power prevents them from seeing much play (not including Yata Garasu).

New Spirit

Spirit monsters are a new type of monster to be introduced in this set. By themselves, they are rather weak as they can't stay on the field for more than a turn and they can't be Special Summoned. However, they make up for it with some rather powerful Effects.

Thankfully, some Magic cards can't help to counter the bad Effects of this monster, such as the Spiritual Energy Settle Machine which will keep your spirit monster from returning to you. Or you could try Spirit's Invitation, which will prevent your opponent from gaining a huge monster advantage on you.

As for the Spirit monsters themselves, you have many high level and lower level monsters to choose. Asura Priest is a nice level four monster, as it can act as a Raigeki for you. Monsters such as Yamata Dragon or Hino-Kagu-Tsuchi can also be very deadly if they are able to damage the opponent.

Warrior Strength

Many strong Warrior monsters as well as warrior-supporting Magic cards were released in LOD. Monsters such as Marauding Captain will let you summon an army very fast, as well as prevent your warrior from being attacked, especially if you can get two Marauding Captains on the field.

In addition, a very powerful monster removal warrior, Exiled Force, was released. The ability of this monster to

SHADOW TAMER

YATA-GARASU

Magician of Faith, so you can pound the magician for a lot of damage.

Fiber Jar will also do nicely in a Beatdown as it can clear the field for you to do a direct attack. However, it may also hurt you if you're using Bazoo or Skull Lair. If you are able to draw a monster, simply flip the Fiber Jar on your turn and the field is clear for your attack.

Helping Hand

Hand Disruption decks were probably the most helped by this set with the release of perhaps the most evil and deadly monster around, Yata-Garasu. Hand Disruption decks are usually able to determine exactly what is in your opponent's hand most of the time with cards such as Forceful Sentry or Confiscation. Also, you don't have to clear the field to play Yata-Garasu. Once you know your opponent has nothing in his hand that can help him, you play Yata-Garasu and it's game over for the opponent. He or she has no option left.

You could also try using Convulsion of Nature. If you know there's something you don't want your opponent to draw next, you can attack with Yata-Garasu and stop them from drawing that card.

Also, you might want to consider using Asura Priest. If you can combo this card with Robbin' Goblin and find a way to damage your opponent using this monster (by either powering it up with Equips or Fairy Meteor

destroy both face up and face down monsters makes in invaluable to prevent harmful flip effects.

You also have support Magic cards such as Reinforcement of the Army which will help you get your army out faster. Plus, The Warrior Returning Alive will help you revive your defeated warrior back for another round.

Beatdown decks didn't get too use much in this set. There were some specialty cards that you could use such as Spear Dragon or Creature Swap, but no outstanding monsters in this deck for you.

Creature Swap is especially nice after you flip a

Crush), you could destroy an entire hand with just Asura Priest.

Exodia and Burn decks didn't get much in this set. Burn decks may be able to use Ominous Fortunetelling for some continuous damage, but the best card that will help these two decks is Fiber Jar. It will let you reuse your Burn cards and it can help revive pieces of Exodia that can't be revived any other way.

Tossing in New Decks

A new deck type that this set may spawn will revolve around Second Coin Toss. This card will convert some previously horrendous cards into something fairly competitive. Examples would include Jirai Gumo or Time Wizard. It can also provide Barrel Dragon with another chance to destroy a monster. You can also combo this with some Trap cards such as Fairy Box or Fiend Comedian.

Fiend Comedian can be especially deadly as it can remove your opponent's entire grave, getting rid of many possible cards that your opponent can revive or get back with something like Magician of Faith.

Finally, a new type of deck that I've started playing recently is Light. The best monster for Light decks so far is Airknight Parshath. If you power this up with Luminous Spark, you've got a one tribute 2400 attack monster with a Fairy Meteor Crush ability. This monster does it all and can give you card advantage. There's also Asura Priest which I mentioned earlier. Plus, Thunder Nyan Nyan will be great for Light Beatdown decks as it gives them a cheap 1900 attack monster.

In closing, this set didn't provide many cards for the old deck types, but rather spawned a new era of decks. That is a welcome addition in an environment that was getting rather stale.

■

Pojo's Legacy of Darkness
DECK DOUBLE REVIEW

Pojo's Ratings:

5 YuGi's	4 YuGi's	3 YuGi's	2 YuGi's	1 YuGi
Killer	Strong	Solid	Iffy	Sucks

Guest Reviewer 1 in Left Column · · · · · Guest Reviewer 2 in Right Column

LOD-000 Yata-Garasu
Reviewed by: SomeGuy.

It's an amazing card. Yata-Garasu can sin-gle handily win you the game. It's not an uncommon sight at all. Yata-Garasu is one of, if not the, most devastating monsters in the game. I could go on and on about it, but I won't. ;)

LOD–000 Yata-Garasu
Reviewed by: Wartortle32

This is probably the most game-changing mon-ster released in the set. If you have cleared your opponent's field and hand, and you play this monster, it's lights out for your opponent. One of the most desired cards in the set. I wouldn't recommend this for decks that don't have hand disruption though.

LOD-001 Dark Ruler Ha Des
Reviewed by: SomeGuy.

Ha Des is one of the better one-tribute monsters currently available in the English version of Duel Monsters. Not only can he destroy Jinzo in one swift attack, Ha Des is also the worst enemy of many effect monsters. Anything that can prevent Witch of the Black Forest from searching out a bigger threat is some good in my book.

LOD–001 Dark Ruler Ha Des
Reviewed by: Wartortle32

For Fiend decks, this is a perfect fit to go along with Dark Necrofear. It has the deadly effect of being able to cancel the effects of monsters that it and your other fiends destroy, thus taking away an important part of the game for your opponent. Plus, the attack is only 50 points less than Summoned Skull and 50 more than the potent Jinzo.

LOD-002 Dark Balter the Terrible
Reviewed by: SomeGuy.

Dark Balter the Terrible is coupled with some extremely powerful Effects. Although the fact that he must be Special Summoned by Fusion lessens his overall potential.

LOD–002 Dark Balter the Terrible
Reviewed by: Wartortle32

This card would have been awesome as a regular monster, but since it is a Fusion, that hurts it a little. However, with the cards released in LoN to help you fuse cards faster, it shouldn't be too big of a problem. The 2000 ATK isn't that great as it will easily be overpowered in todays metagame. Overall, it's rather weak and I wouldn't bother considering this in any deck.

LOD-003 Lesser Fiend
Reviewed by: SomeGuy.

Lesser Fiend is definitely not worth the Tribute. His pathetic stats and below average Effect hardly make him playable. There are much better options available.

LOD–003 Lesser Fiend
Reviewed by: Wartortle32

When combined with Ha Des, this is a very annoying card. Not only do the opponent's monsters not get their effects, they won't be able to revive them either. But with only 2100 attack for a level five monster, it isn't too powerful. You'll have to boost it up with some Equip cards if you want it to survive for a few turns.

LOD-004 Possessed Dark Soul
Reviewed by: SomeGuy.

If Clown Control is big in your area, this is a great counter. A permanent Change of Heart for all of your opponent's level three and under monsters can potentially be very powerful. Keep in mind that it's not very good versus the average Beatdown deck.

LOD–004 Possessed Dark Soul
Reviewed by: Wartortle32

I don't see this as being too useful. Your opponent won't run many good level three or less monsters unless he's using some sort of Stall / Jinzo #7 deck. In that case, it would be very useful. I wouldn't consider this any better than a Side Deck card.

LOD-005 Winged Minion
Reviewed by: SomeGuy.

Winged Minion is an extremely unplayable card. Tributing one of your own monsters in order to give another Fiend Monster +700 ATK/DEF is one of the worst Effects I've ever seen. Stick to your basic Equipment Magic cards.

LOD-005 Winged Minion
Reviewed by: Wartortle32

Not a very good card. There's much better for your deck in here.

LOD-006 Skull Knight #2
Reviewed by: SomeGuy.

Skull Knight #2 is only decent when used as Tribute fodder. The problem is that most competitive decks run little Tribute Monsters. Not to mention the fact that Skull Knight #2's stats are horrible.

LOD–006 Skull Knight #2
Reviewed by: Wartortle32

This card would be good in a Fiend deck. It gives you a free summon, which you can take advantage of with United We Stand or something similar. The attack isn't strong though, so if you leave it in attack mode, it will get pummeled.

LOD-007 Ryu-Kishin Clown
Reviewed by: SomeGuy.

Wow, these stats are disgusting. 800/500 ATK/DEF isn't going to get you anywhere. Plus, add in the fact that his Effect is useless and we have another horrible Monster.

LOD–007 Ryu-Kishin Clown
Reviewed by: Wartortle32

Another addition to Clown decks becomes available. I don't consider this clown to be up to the standards of Dream Clown or Crass Clown, as it doesn't give you monster advantage. Its ATK is also weaker than the other clowns. I personally wouldn't use this card unless it's in a Casual Clown deck.

LOD-008 Twin-Headed Wolf
Reviewed by: SomeGuy.

This card is decent, but not good enough to be used in a Fiend deck. Since it needs another Fiend monster on the field for it to be effective, it's too easy to disrupt. Stick to Dark Ruler Ha Des.

LOD–008 Twin-Headed Wolf
Reviewed by: Wartortle32

With only 1500 attack, it won't survive long without some sort of power up. It's Effect is very nice by taking care of troublesome Flip Effect monsters such as Cyber Jar or Fiber Jar. It's definitely a very good card for Fiend decks.

LOD-009 Opticlops
Reviewed by: SomeGuy.

Opticlops is the new La Jinn the Mystical Genie of the Lamp with better stats. This is a card to consider in a straight casual Fiend deck.

LOD–009 Opticlops
Reviewed by: Wartortle32

This monster provides Fiend decks with another strong level four monster. It gives you another option to La Jinn as this has a stronger defense. However, the higher defense means that it can't be searched for by the Witch. There's room for both cards in Fiend decks, as there is a lack of strong Fiend monsters.

LOD-010 Bark of Dark Ruler
Reviewed by: SomeGuy.

This isn't a very good Trap card. Bark of Dark Ruler has the potential to catch your opponent off guard, but I don't like the fact that you have to pay Life Points for it. There are better Trap cards to occupy your deck space.

LOD–010 Bark of Dark Ruler
Reviewed by: Wartortle32

I don't think this card is that great. It would be easier to use regular attack and def boosts such as Rush Recklessly as those don't have a cost. I suppose you could cause massive damage with this, but you would probably be taking just as much damage as you give. Perhaps if you are really ahead in LP, it might be useful to finish off your opponent. It wouldn't work in close games.

LOD-011 Fatal Abacus
Reviewed by: SomeGuy.

All Fatal Abacus does is give you a benefit for winning. Obviously if you are winning, you don't need small benefits like this card. The other use it has is against Recursion decks. However, those decks aren't currently very powerful.

LOD–011 Fatal Abacus
Reviewed by: Wartortle32

I don't see much use for this card. It's like a specialized Skull Invitation, which isn't good itself. I guess if you're in the lead and you have your opponent on the defense, this helps kill him or her quicker. However, in that scenario, you're probably far in the lead and will win anyway. There are better cards to use.

LOD-012 Life Absorbing Machine
Reviewed by: SomeGuy.

This Trap actually has some solid potential. The most obvious use would be in a casual Toon deck or an Exodia deck. Both of which could use the card to its maximum potential.

LOD–012 Life Absorbing Machine
Reviewed by: Wartortle32

This takes the bite out of the hefty cost of Dark Elf, Solemn Judgment or other LP payment cards. Now you only have to pay 1/4 of your LP for Solemn and only 500 LP for Elf. If you run a deck that has a lot of cost cards (Toon decks), this is a very nice card to have. Note however that this is for LP paid, not lost by other reasons.

LOD-013 The Puppet Magic of Dark Ruler
Reviewed by: SomeGuy.

This card is what I call crappy recursion. The amount you have to pay to Special Summon a monster from your Graveyard is enormous. Who really wants to Raigeki themselves for a single monster? It may have some mediocre uses in the future.

LOD–013 The Puppet Magic of Dark Ruler
Reviewed by: Wartortle32

This card requires too much chance for it to be good. The best Fiend monster that can be revived is Summoned Skull. It's very difficult to find the right monsters whose combined level is exactly the same as the level of the Fiend you are reviving. I suppose that the best use of this card would be to trade one monster of a level for another monster with the same level.

LOD-014 Soul Demolition
Reviewed by: SomeGuy.

Wow, what a pointless Trap card! Even if you didn't have to pay the measly 500 Life Points to activate it, it still wouldn't be very useful against the majority of deck types on the scene.

LOD–014 Soul Demolition
Reviewed by: Wartortle32

Maybe I'm missing something, but I don't see a use for thi card. Perhaps if you know your opponent has Monster Reborn and you could remove all the monsters from his grave, you could use it. However, it isn't worth 500 LP per monster, since the opponent gets to choose which monster to remove. I see a possibility of using a combo with Graverobber's Retribution, but it's not going to do enough damage to be effective.

LOD-015 Double Snare
Reviewed by: SomeGuy.

Double Snare might as well read, "Destroy a face-up Jinzo on the field". Because that's the main use you will be getting out of it. Although, that Effect still doesn't make it worth using in any deck. It's much too situational.

LOD–015 Double Snare
Reviewed by: Wartortle32

I'm sure you're all thinking the main use o this card is to kill Jinzo. However, this card is limited in its use. There are only a few cards this card can destroy. You're better off using regular monster removal Magic cards or strong monsters to destroy Jinzo.

LOD-016 Freed the Matchless General
Reviewed by: SomeGuy.

Freed the Matchless General is not bad in some Warrior based decks. Most versions of Warrior Beatdown don't need him. If he had 500 more ATK, I'm sure he would get more playability. One-Tribute 2300 ATK doesn't cut it with Goblin Attack Force running around.

LOD–016 Freed the Matchless General
Reviewed by: Wartortle32

This card's Effect is really good if you're running low on monsters or you just need one more monster to do a one turn KO with a bunch of monsters. The Effect prevents your opponent from snatch stealing it or using Change of Heart. Many players will forget this ability and try to target it with Magic cards. I would consider this a staple for Warrior decks.

LOD-017 Throwstone Unit
Reviewed by: SomeGuy.

Throwstone Unit isn't too bad of a defender, but it's not going to be easy to obtain multiple Warrior monsters on the field to utilize his Effect. With all the Monster Removal within Duel Monsters, keeping more than two steady monsters on the field is a challenge.

LOD–017 Throwstone Unit
Reviewed by: Wartortle32

With only 900 attack, you'll only use it to destroy Gemini elves, GAFs or other 1800 attack monsters. However with a single power up, you can destroy Jinzo or Summoned Skull and a bunch o other powerful monsters. At the very least, the high defense should replace all those other Level Four 2000 defense monsters you might be using.

Pojo's UNOFFICIAL Guide to Legacy of Darkness

This book is not sponsored, endorsed, or otherwise affiliated with any of the companies or products featured in this book. This is not an official publication.

LOD-018 Marauding Captain
Reviewed by: SomeGuy.

Marauding Captain is easily the best Warrior to come out of Legacy of Darkness. Not only does he have one great Effect, he has a second one to boot. Don't judge him by his low ATK; this monster can do some pretty amazing tricks.

👁️ 👁️ 👁️ 👁️

LOD–018 Marauding Captain
Reviewed by: Wartortle32

It provides a good defense for your other Warriors, but with only 1200 attack, it needs a Mage Power or a United We Stand to protect it. It should be an option for you if you're using the weaker Warrior monsters. The best part of this card is that if you have two copies out, and all of your monsters are Warriors, your opponent will be unable to attack at all. The Effect of letting you summon another level four monster is great for Beatdown as it gives you another strong attacker.

👁️ 👁️ 👁️ 👁️

LOD-019 Ryu Senshi
Reviewed by: SomeGuy.

Ryu Senshi isn't a bad card. It's the Fusion that kills it. When you add in the fact that it has to be fused, Ryu Senshi no longer is any good.

👁️ 👁️

LOD–019 Ryu Senshi
Reviewed by: Wartortle32

With a Seven Tools Effect, this monster can provide your other Warrior protection from Mirror Force and those other nasty traps. It's a Fusion monster with only 2000 attack, which makes it almost unplayable since he's difficult to summon and can be easily destroyed by an attack.

👁️ 👁️ 👁️

LOD-020 Warrior Dai Grepher
Reviewed by: SomeGuy.

It's a basic, Effect less 1700 ATK Monster. There is nothing to be amazed about it. Much better alternatives are available.

👁️ 👁️

LOD–020 Warrior Dai Grepher
Reviewed by: Wartortle32

This monster has no Effect and 1700 attack. With the large amount of Warrior monsters already out, there's no reason to use this card even in a Warrior deck. I suppose this could be a cheap substitute if you don't have the money to get more rare Warriors.

👁️

LOD-021 Mysterious Guard
Reviewed by: SomeGuy.

Mysterious Guard is an interesting card. Not only can it be like a Penguin Soldier, but it can also screw with your opponent's next two draws. It's not bad at all…

👁️ 👁️

LOD–021 Mysterious Guard
Reviewed by: Wartortle32

This card is similar to Penguin Soldier, but it's hurt by the fact that it can only return face up monsters. The ability to return to the top of the deck makes it similar to a powered up Time Seal. Given that it can only return face up monsters, I would personally stick with the Penguin Soldier.

👁️ 👁️ 👁️

LOD-022 Frontier Wiseman
Reviewed by: SomeGuy.

Frontier Wiseman has a good Effect, but how often are you going to have many other monsters on your side of the field? Seeing how it only benefits Warriors, it doesn't work in a large variety of decks.

LOD–022 Frontier Wiseman
Reviewed by: Wartortle32

This monster protects your Warriors from targeted Magic cards. This includes Equip cards as well as cards like Change of Heart or Tribute to the Doomed. The stats for this monster are very good considering that it's a level three. But it's still weak compared to most monsters, so your opponent can simply attack it first before using any Magic cards. It's not too useful unless you power it up with some non-targeted Magic cards.

LOD-023 Exiled Force
Reviewed by: SomeGuy.

Exiled Force is the best targeted monster removal that any deck can abuse. For the simple price of skipping your regular Summon for the turn, you can destroy any monster on the field. It's extremely solid.

LOD–023 Exiled Force
Reviewed by: Wartortle32

This monster is limited to one in Japan and I expect the same will apply here. It's a great way to destroy really powered up monsters or perhaps a Jinzo that is stopping all your Traps. What is really good about this card is that it can take Flip Effect monsters without activating their Effect. It's also easy to get this monster out with Sangan, WotBF, Freed the Undefeated General or Reinforcement of the Army.

LOD-024 The Hunter with 7 Weapons
Reviewed by: SomeGuy.

The Hunter with 7 Weapons is too situational to be any good. There are also other ways to achieve the equivalent of 2000 ATK.

LOD–024 The Hunter with 7 Weapons
Reviewed by: Wartortle32

This card is more of a Side Deck card. It's not really useful until you know what kind of monsters the opponent is using. Even then, it isn't that good as most decks won't only be using 1 type of monster.

LOD-025 Shadow Tamer
Reviewed by: SomeGuy.

Shadow Tamer is like a restricted Change of Heart. It can only impact Fiend monsters. It's another situational card. Not to mention the fact that it's a Monster card rather than a Magic card.

LOD–025 Shadow Tamer
Reviewed by: Wartortle32

Another situational card. There aren't enough strong Fiends currently for this to be good. Most of the time, you won't even see a Fiend in the entire duel. There's going to be a much better card named XENO in the next set that lets you take control of any monster for a turn. By the time you are reading this, it will most likely be available. It's much more versatile than this card.

LOD-026 Dragon Manipulator
Reviewed by: NickWhiz1

This card is only as useful as the number of dragons in your opponent's deck. Since Spear Dragon is popular, I suppose you could try this on it. However, it's only effective if you Flip Summon it. This limitation knocks it down, like, a lot.

LOD–026 Dragon Manipulator
Reviewed by: Wartortle32

This is the dragon version of the card listed above. Dragon decks are going to be a lot more popular than Fiends, so this may be a little better than the Shadow Tamer. Still, I wouldn't use this for anything more than a Side deck card.

LOD-027 The A. Forces
Reviewed by: NickWhiz1

A 200 attack point boost doesn't really matter much in this game. Even if you manage to get three or four Warriors/Spellcasters on the field (which is almost impossible, considering you'll be lucky to maintain two), it's not really worth it. All it takes is one little M/T removal to nuke it.

LOD–027 The A. Forces
Reviewed by: Wartortle32

This card is like a Field Magic card for Warriors. Usually in play you're only going to have one or two Warriors or Spellcasters on the field. Maybe three tops. Monsters don't survive long in today's environment. So you're looking at maybe 200-400 attack boost. I don't think it is worth it. You're better off going with the regular equip attack boosts such as Mage Power or United We Stand. If you can't afford those rare Equip cards, this might be a good option for Warrior decks.

LOD-028 Reinforcement of the Army
Reviewed by: NickWhiz1

Now this is a card that is actually useful! Need to pull out that Exiled Force, Goblin Attack Force, or Marauding Captain? All you have to do is slap this thing down, and you get it instantly. Expect it to be restricted to two, if it isn't already.

LOD–028 Reinforcement of the Army
Reviewed by: Wartortle32

This card is restricted to two in Japan, so you can expect the same here. There were a lot of good Warrior monsters released in this set, so this card will be abused in Warrior decks. It is perfect for retrieving monsters like Exiled Force or Marauding Captain.

LOD-029 Array of Revealing Light
Reviewed by: NickWhiz1

You know, I've seen this card before. Oh yeah, it was called "Vengeful Bog Spirit". The difference is that this card only effects one type, which is declared at activation. Personally, I'd rather destroy my opponent's monsters than not let them attack. Plus, what guarantee is there that he or she will only have one type of monster on the field?

LOD–029 Array of Revealing Light
Reviewed by: Wartortle32

This is more of a Side deck card. Once you know what kind of deck you're going up against, then you can main deck it. It's like a specialized Vengeful Bog Spirit. Still, it will only hold your opponent for so long. All this does is prevent any fast break one turn KO of your LP, unless your opponent destroys this Magic card.

LOD-030 The Warrior Returning Alive
Reviewed by: NickWhiz1

I suppose you could use this as some type of pseudo-recursion. It's not that bad. I think this card works best with Marauding Captain, because MC can swarm. A good second choice is Exiled Force.

👁👁👁

LOD–030 The Warrior Returning Alive
Reviewed by: Wartortle32

Unlike Calling Reinforcements, this card can get any warrior monster. With a lot of great warriors being released like Exiled Force, this will have a spot in warrior decks along with Calling Reinforcements.

👁👁👁

LOD-031 Ready for Intercepting
Reviewed by: NickWhiz1

If you want to reuse Magician of Faith, just play this card for a free second use. Then again, who uses Magician of Faith these days? I don't know many people who do, because Fiber Jar does the same thing about a hundred times better.

👁👁

LOD–031 Ready for Intercepting
Reviewed by: Wartortle32

The only thing this is good for is to reuse Flip Effect monsters. The only playable card to use with it would be Magician of Faith. Perhaps as a secondary Effect, you could put a weak monster in defense so that you don't lose a lot of LP if it's attacked.

👁👁

LOD-032 A Feint Plan
Reviewed by: NickWhiz1

If you want to protect your face-downs, use Waboku. They'll still be flipped over if they're attacked, but they won't die. Waboku protects face-ups and is more versatile. Only use this card if you're really, really worried about not getting Cyber/Fiber Jar to your advantage.

👁👁

LOD–032 A Feint Plan
Reviewed by: Wartortle32

The best that you can do with this card is stall for a turn if you happen to have a face down monster. I see no use for this card when you can just use a Waboku. It's much more versatile as it will protect your monsters, whether they are face up or face down, as well as your LP. There is no reason to use this card over Waboku or any other attack prevention Trap.

👁👁

LOD-033 Emergency Provisions
Reviewed by: NickWhiz1

Eh, I can see how this card can be useful, but only if you're about to get a lot of your M/T removed. You can chain to it and sell off all your M/T for 1000 LP apiece before they're destroyed. I still think it's not game-breaking, though it's not bad either.

👁👁👁

LOD–033 Emergency Provisions
Reviewed by: Wartortle32

This might be good in a LP Gain deck. It works against Heavy Storm by letting you clear off your M/T so you gain some LP. Or you could use it to clean off some of your M/T zone, letting you play or set more cards.

👁👁👁

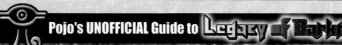

LOD-034 Tyrant Dragon
Reviewed by: NickWhiz1

Let's see…Magic Cylinder can't touch it, it has the capability to attack twice, why would I not play it? Oh yeah, there's that part about offering a dragon just to Special Summon it from the Graveyard. Of course, if it's in the Graveyard, you probably messed up anyway. Very Lord of D. combo-able.

LOD–034 Tyrant Dragon
Reviewed by: Wartortle32

This monster works well as a field clearing attacker. Unfortunately, it can't attack again if there are no monsters left on your opponent's side of the field. It's still very good in a Dragon deck. I wouldn't suggest it other than in a Dragon deck as the sacrificial dragon required to Special Summon this monster really hurts it.

LOD-035 Spear Dragon
Reviewed by: NickWhiz1

The second English 1900, and it even has trample! (M:TG term for the Fairy Meteor Crush effect). The switching to defense part is annoying, but unlike GAF, it can change next turn! This card even pops up in Warrior decks, so it must be good.

LOD–03 Spear Dragon
Reviewed by: Wartortle32

The new 1900 attack monster is Spear Dragon. This monster works wonders against Flip Effect monsters, Scapegoats, or GAFs in defense. Since it can change back to attack mode the next turn, you only have to protect it for one turn. You can use something like Waboku or Magic Cylinder before it can attack again, whereas you have to protect GAF for two turns.

LOD-036 Spirit Ryu
Reviewed by: NickWhiz1

Ick, this card tells Hand Advantage to go screw itself. I suppose you could discard a Blue-Eyes or something, then revive it later, but there are more efficient ways to do it (Graceful Charity, Painful Choice, etc.)

LOD–036 Spirit Ryu
Reviewed by: Wartortle32

This monster's Effect, while good, is very costly. If you plan to use this card, I suggest you don't use the Effect until you're planning to go on a full out one turn KO. Discarding from your hand is never good, and when the result is only a 1000 boost, it isn't worth it in the long run.

LOD-037 The Dragon Dwelling in the Cave
Reviewed by: NickWhiz1

Giant Soldier of Stone turned into a dragon, and this is how he ends up. This guy is level four, though, so he can't do the same things. It works nicely in a Shield & Sword deck, but how many of those exist these days? =/

LOD–037 The Dragon Dwelling in the Cave
Reviewed by: Wartortle32

Not much to say about this card. It gives a 2000 def monster for dragons. I wouldn't use it as there are already many 2000 def monsters around.

LOD-038 Lizard Soldier
Reviewed by: NickWhiz1

Ick, a plain monster. Stay away.

LOD-038 Lizard Soldier
Reviewed by: Wartortle32

This is one of the required useless cards that has to be released in every set. Don't ever use this card.

LOD-039 Fiend Skull Dragon
Reviewed by: NickWhiz1

This is the weakest of the three cross-type Fusions. Although it has a built-in Royal Command and can't be targeted by Traps, it's not really worth it. The two cards used to fuse for it aren't that bad, really.

LOD-039 Fiend Skull Dragon
Reviewed by: Wartortle32

This isn't a very good monster. Its attack is only 2000 and you get the same effect with Royal Command. Plus, there aren't even many targeted Traps besides Magic Cylinder, so that second Effect isn't much use.

LOD-040 Cave Dragon
Reviewed by: NickWhiz1

The first (and only) Level Four 2000 Dragon, and it's not horrid. Notice how it says you can't Normal Summon it if you have other monsters. It doesn't mean you can't Flip Summon or Special Summon it. Also, you'll probably be using this in a Dragon deck, so the second Effect isn't all bad. All-in-all, a surprisingly good monster.

LOD-040 Cave Dragon
Reviewed by: Wartortle32

Obviously, you shouldn't consider this card outside a Dragon deck. Even then, it isn't that great as it's going to be hard to summon this monster. Fortunately, you can Special Summon this monster if there is a monster on your field, so it isn't entirely unplayable.

LOD-041 Gray Wing
Reviewed by: NickWhiz1

Uhhh, yeah, I don't get this card. Hayabusa Knight has 300 less attack, but he doesn't require a discard. It's debatable which one has more combo support, but I would stick with Hayabusa.

LOD-041 Gray Wing
Reviewed by: Wartortle32

This monster is like a Hayabusa, with 300 more attack. The 300 will not make much of a difference, so I see little reason to use this card over Hayabusa. The cost of discarding won't be a problem if you can discard something like Sinister Serpent, but I would still stick with Hayabusa.

LOD-042 Troop Dragon
Reviewed by: NickWhiz1

Wow, someone at Konami messed up! Originally, this Effect would only go off if it were destroyed in battle. Now if it's destroyed in any way, another one comes to take its place. It's become somewhat playable. The stats are nothing to write home about, however, and Nimble is still better. It isn't that bad. Seriously, it isn't.

LOD–042 Troop Dragon
Reviewed by: Wartortle32

This monster is simply a pesky monster, and a great defender early in the game. It can be helpful to get you another Tribute to summon a high level monster. Still, its weak attack makes it a very tough monster to fit into a competitive deck.

LOD-043 The Dragon's Bead
Reviewed by: NickWhiz1

Ick. This is one of the worst rares in the entire game. I'm not kidding. If it negated the Trap cards without a discard, it would be quite playable. As it stands, however, it works well as rare toilet paper.

LOD–043 The Dragon's Bead
Reviewed by: Wartortle32

There aren't many good targeting Traps, which makes this card sub-par. I would just stick to 7 Tools which negates any Trap and can be used against any monster, not just dragons.

LOD-044 A Wingbeat of Giant Dragon
Reviewed by: NickWhiz1

This card isn't worth it unless you are using your opponent's monster (under your control) to activate it. If you are, then by all means use this card! However, it happens very rarely, so steer away. It's still better than The Dragon's Bead, however.

LOD–044 A Wingbeat of Giant Dragon
Reviewed by: Wartortle32

Unless you use Change of Heart or a similar stealing card, you'll be returning your own monster most of the time. Moreover, since the dragon has to be at least level five, you're going to lose a lot of monster advantage. There are already plenty of M/T removal in the game. The only possible use I see for this card is to return a high level spirit type dragon, as it's going to return to your hand anyway.

LOD-045 Dragon's Gunfire
Reviewed by: NickWhiz1

This is an unusual card because it gives you two choices for its Effect. The first choice is basically Ookazi, and the second one can be used to destroy Goblin Attack Force, Spear Dragon, or some weenie monsters, but it's not worth it. Seriously, it isn't. There are better cards.

LOD–045 Dragon's Gunfire
Reviewed by: Wartortle32

This isn't that useful of a card because not too many good monsters have 800 def or less, other than Goblin Attack Force or Spear Dragon. The second effect isn't that great either as 800 damage won't make much of a difference in a duel.

LOD-046 Stamping Destruction
Reviewed by: NickWhiz1

Interesting, a Normal Magic version of Mystical Space Typhoon that can do 500 damage to your opponent. You can see where this is going. Don't play it. MST is infinitely better. 500 damage won't make much of a difference anyway.

👁👁

LOD–046 Stamping Destruction
Reviewed by: Wartortle32

This is a nice card. It's kind of like MST, but it isn't quickplay. However, it makes up for it by doing some damage in the process. A good card for any Dragon deck.

👁👁👁

LOD-047 Super Rejuvenation
Reviewed by: NickWhiz1

Wow, this is actually a decent card! Discarding that dragon with Graceful Charity to recurse it? Draw a card. Offer that Spear Dragon? Draw a card. Played correctly, this card can gain you up to three to four cards. However, it is very situational.

👁👁👁

LOD–047 Super Rejuvenation
Reviewed by: Wartortle32

This card lets you draw one card for each dragon monster you discard or tribute during the same turn. It isn't permanent, so use it when you have discarded or tributed two or more. It may be too hard when you have a strong dragon like Tyrant Dragon. Or you may discard a dragon for something like Tribute to the Doomed or Magic Jammer. You definitely don't want to use this card when you have only got rid of one dragon as that wouldn't give you much card advantage.

👁👁👁

LOD-048 Dragon's Rage
Reviewed by: NickWhiz1

Another nice dragon support card. This gives all of your dragons a Fairy Meteor Crush/Trample effect. That means that your Tyrant Dragon can get off two attacks of 2900 in Trampling power, etc. Yowzers. Obviously doesn't work with Spear Dragon, as it already has Trample =P

👁👁👁

LOD–048 Dragon's Rage
Reviewed by: Wartortle32

This goes very nice in a Dragon deck. Imagine staring down two BEWD with this card active on the field. Not a pretty sight. It probably belongs in any offensive Dragon deck.

👁👁👁👁

LOD-049 Burst Breath
Reviewed by: NickWhiz1

OK, this card is screaming to be abused. Not with the predictable choices like Spear Dragon and stuff, but by Twin-Headed Behemoth. 1500 is enough to kill off almost every popular monster, and it even comes back! This card can be very dangerous if used correctly. Torrential Tribute still beats it, however =/

👁👁👁

LOD–049 Burst Breath
Reviewed by: Wartortle32

This could act like a Raigeki, and is a great way of getting rid of high attack and low defense monsters like Summoned Skull. You should consider it if you're using a Dragon deck.

👁👁👁

LOD-050 Luster Dragon
Reviewed by: NickWhiz1

Finally, we get a decent one-tribute drag-on! One tribute for 2400/1400 is very economical. You can always use the Lord of D. combo, although it's better reserved for Tyrant Dragon/BEWD.

LOD–050 Luster Dragon
Reviewed by: Wartortle32

I don't see much use for this card. We already have plenty of one tribute 2400 attack monsters. It doesn't have an Effect, so Dragon deck users may just pass on this card.

LOD-051 Robotic Knight
Reviewed by: NickWhiz1

You can always tell where the first Japanese set ends and the next one begins, because sets normally begin with a couple of crappy monsters. This is one of them. 1600/1800, while not bad, it's just not good enough.

LOD-051 Robotic Knight
Reviewed by: Raymond Purnama (a.k.a. TwInSeN21)

A decent Machine monster. If you are play-ing a Machine deck and can't afford Mechanicalchasers, you might want to consider playing this card for its high defense and decent attack.

LOD-052 Wolf Axwielder
Reviewed by: NickWhiz1

Ehhhh......no.

LOD-052 Wolf Axeweilder
Reviewed by: Raymond Purnama (a.k.a. TwInSeN21)

If you are playing a Warrior Deck, you should try and get Axe Raiders instead since it has 50 more ATK. This card is decent, it's just that there are better cards available.

LOD-053 The Illusionary Gentleman
Reviewed by: NickWhiz1

Ehhhh......no.

LOD-053 The Illusory Gentleman
Reviewed by: Raymond Purnama (a.k.a. TwInSeN21)

Meh. There are way better Spellcasters (like Gemini Elf) or Dark monsters out there. This is the type of card that you don't play unless you can't get anything better.

LOD-054 Robolady
Reviewed by: NickWhiz1

Ehhhh......no.

LOD-054 Robolady
Reviewed by: Raymond Purnama (a.k.a. TwInSeN21)

This card is just plain horrible. The stats suck and the Fusion is dreadful. If for some reason you want to play the Fusion, try and get some Fusion Substitutes instead (which you can get from the Tournament Packs).

LOD-055 Roboyarou
Reviewed by: NickWhiz1

Ehhhh......no.

LOD-055 Roboyarou
Reviewed by: Raymond Purnama (a.k.a. TwInSeN21)

Slightly better stats than Robolady, but still nowhere near playable. Most of the comments made about Robolady apply to Roboyarou as well. Don't bother with this pair.

LOD-056 Fiber Jar
Reviewed by: NickWhiz1

Ehhhh......wait, this is a good card! A very good card! A near-staple, in fact! Fiber Jar is the most famous of the Jars, because of its reset ability. The term "soft reset" has been applied to this monster, because it resets everything except LP and cards removed from the game. Very, very good.

LOD-056 Fiber Jar
Reviewed by: Raymond Purnama (a.k.a. TwInSeN21)

One of the most game breaking Flip effects out there. It basically lets you restart your game except for LP and cards removed from the game. It's a lot more reliable than Cyber Jar (unless you run a lot of Bazoo The Soul-Eaters, Skull Lairs, etc). If your opponent attacks your face down Fiber Jar, it means that he skips his Battle Phase and enters Main Phase 2. If you Flip Summon it during your turn in Main Phase 1, you get an open field to attack. It also shuffles back cards from the graveyard that are otherwise hard to get back (like Spirit Monsters and Exodia Pieces).

LOD-057 Serpentine Princess
Reviewed by: NickWhiz1

Another monster with a unique Effect. This monster appears to combo best with the card right before it (Fiber Jar). The field will reset, except you have a monster on your side of the field. It may not be worth it. Much better than other 2000 defenders, though.

LOD-057 Serpentine Princess
Reviewed by: Raymond Purnama (a.k.a. TwInSeN21)

A good card with high defense. The Effect can also be abused if you run cards like Penguin Soldiers and Fiber Jar. 1400ATK also means that it will finally replace Giant Soldier of Stone in some decks that still rely on heavy defense.

Pojo's UNOFFICIAL Guide to Legacy of Darkness

This book is not sponsored, endorsed by, or otherwise affiliated with any of the companies or products featured in this book. This is not an official publication.

LOD-058 Patrician of Darkness
Reviewed by: NickWhiz1

Until we get Vampire Lord, this is the most powerful Zombie monster (Shadow Ghoul is too situational). Its Effect is not bad at all. You can redirect the attack of your opponent to a higher attack monster, or in Pharaonic Guardian, to the Spirit Soul Hunter, which can't be destroyed by battle. It equals a negated attack. This may be one of the harder hitters in a Zombie deck until we get Vampire Lord.

LOD-058 Patrician of Darkness
Reviewed by: Raymond Purnama (a.k.a. TwInSeN21)

This card's Effect can be devastating (especially when Zombie decks become more playable). Unfortunately 2000ATK can be considered quite low for a one Tribute Monster, as we are so used to cards like Jinzo and Summoned Skull.

LOD-059 Thunder Nyan Nyan
Reviewed by: NickWhiz1

Another Level Four 1900, but harder to play. You can only get away with it in a mono-Light deck, unless you stick it on the field by itself. It's not bad, just highly situational. However, this is the easiest Level Four 1900 to find, being only a Rare.

LOD-059 Thunder Nyan Nyan
Reviewed by: Raymond Purnama (a.k.a. TwInSeN21)

What else can I say? Only play this card in a Light Deck (unless you have quite a few Light Monsters). Otherwise, it's better to play Gemini Elf as it is more reliable. Thunder Nyan Nyan's Effect is best when your opponent tries to gain control of her, only to realize that he has non-Light Monsters on the field…

LOD-060 Gradius' Option
Reviewed by: NickWhiz1

This isn't a bad card, although it requires you to play the mediocre Gradius card. However, Gradius has a decent amount of support, including Cyclon Laser, Limiter Removal, and Shining Angel. If you pump up Gradius, you can use this monster as a clone to it. Too bad if one of them is destroyed, they both die.

LOD-060 Gradius' Option
Reviewed by: Raymond Purnama (a.k.a. TwInSeN21)

Obviously you only want to play this if you run a Gradius deck. Get one Gradius on the field, Special Summon all three Gradius' Options from your hand and play Limiter Removal for a one hit kill. I wouldn't really recommend playing this deck unless you are playing for fun.

LOD-061 Woodland Sprite
Reviewed by: NickWhiz1

Yuck, I just don't like this card. It's not worth wasting an Equip card just for 500 damage.

LOD-061 Woodland Sprite
Reviewed by: Raymond Purnama (a.k.a. TwInSeN21)

I guess you can run a weird lock that uses this card's Effect to win. Simply play this with Equips that go back to the top of your deck (like Sword of Deep Seated) and deal a constant 500 damage every turn. It's not very good though.

LOD-062 Airknight Parshath
Reviewed by: NickWhiz1

I still don't get why this card is so popular, but it seems to be somewhat powerful. If it was level four, it would be restricted to one and have some kind of negative effect. However, at one tribute, it's quite balanced. A Level Five 1900 attacker with Trample and Masked Sorcerer, it's pretty good. Just watch out for Goblin Attack Force =/

LOD-062 Airknight Parshath
Reviewed by: Raymond Purnama (a.k.a. TwInSeN21)

One of the best one Tributes in the current environment. A 1900 with built in Fairy Meteor Crush that lets you draw a card whenever it deals damage. This is simply amazing. As you know, cards like Scapegoat and Magician of Faith are really popular, so this card is just a plain beatstick. Card advantage is an important concept in this card game. The card's main problem is its weak attack

LOD-063 Twin-Headed Behemoth
Reviewed by: NickWhiz1

Honestly, this card isn't worth being restricted. I mean, while 1500 ATK for a level three is insane, and it can recover itself at 1000/1000, it's not anything extremely game-breaking. I suppose it can counter monster removal, but, ehh. The only reason it'll be restricted is because its Effect says it can only be used once per duel. Fiber Jar would cause holy hell by having to keep track of more than one of these.

LOD-063 Twin-Headed Behemoth
Reviewed by: Raymond Purnama (a.k.a. TwInSeN21)

This card was restricted in Japan. It was hard to keep track of which copy of the card used the Effect in case a Fiber Jar was flipped. It has a pretty good Effect as it lets you get your Tribute monsters out easier. However, people have been using Monsters like Nimble Momonga for a similar Effect for quite a while now. Note that even if it is destroyed by an effect like Dark Hole, you still get to use the Effect unlike Nimbles.

LOD-064 Maharaghi
Reviewed by: NickWhiz1

This is one of the few cards that can control the next card you draw. Although it's not worth wasting your Normal Summon on it, especially since it only has stats of 1200/1700.

LOD-064 Maharaghi
Reviewed by: Raymond Purnama (a.k.a. TwInSeN21)

An interesting Spirit Monster. It improves your draw at the cost of your normal Summon for the turn. I don't see this card being too playable, as no one really plays with cards like Big Eye and Ancient Telescope.

LOD-065 Inaba White Rabbit
Reviewed by: NickWhiz1

One of the more useful Spirits. A 700 ATK direct attacker is quite good. Try using it in Fire Princess or Clown Control and let the cute little rabbit poke your opponent.

LOD-065 Inaba White Rabit
Reviewed by: Raymond Purnama (a.k.a. TwInSeN21)

I think this card has some potential. It's a Spirit Monster that can attack directly. One of the main problems with direct attackers is that they have low attacks. Without any protection, your opponent is likely to kill them at the next turn. This card goes back to your hand at the end of turn, making it immune to attacks and Spell Speed 1 Effects. As long as you can find a way to protect your LP (like Messenger of Peace and Gravity Bind), you can just keep on attacking for 700 damage every turn. Add an Equip or two and the damage will pile up very quickly.

LOD-066 Susa Soldier
Reviewed by: NickWhiz1

This is an underrated card. While it is a Spirit and it only does half damage to your opponent, it's still a Level 4 2000. In a dedicated Spirit deck (with Spiritual Energy Settle Machine), this card can be dangerous. It must be halfway decent, it was an Ultra/Parallel Rare in Japanese =/

LOD-066 Susa Soldier
Reviewed by: Raymond Purnama (a.k.a. TwInSeN21)

This is a mediocre card at best. First of all, you can't use Witch to fetch it and it does less damage if it attacks directly. You can use it as a board clearer, but I'd use Asura Priest instead.

LOD-067 Yamata Dragon
Reviewed by: NickWhiz1

Any Spirits that require Tributes are not worth it. Yes, it gives you draw power and card advantage, but you have to Tribute two monsters to summon it out. It also only lasts for one turn. Any field advantage you get is totally screwed.

LOD-067 Yamata Dragon
Reviewed by: Raymond Purnama (a.k.a. TwInSeN21)

The ability to draw 5 cards might seem amazing at first, until you realize how hard is it to actually Normal Summon a 2 Tribute Monster, especially when cards like Trap Hole, Bottomless Trap Hole and Torrential Tribute are quite popular. Being a Spirit Monster, the fact that the card comes back to your hand at the end of the turn is bad as well, considering all of the trouble you went through to get it out. At least it's better than Hino-Kagu-Tsuchi...

LOD-068 Great Long Nose
Reviewed by: NickWhiz1

Ick. Airknight Parshath is a MUCH more useful Level Five 1900, and it's not even a Spirit. Now, if this card had Trample (FMC effect), it might be SLIGHTLY useful, but, uhh, stay away.

LOD-068 Great Long Nose
Reviewed by: Raymond Purnama (a.k.a. TwInSeN21)

An amusing name, but that's all it offers. The card's Effect is pretty good, but being a one tribute Spirit is its downfall. You shouldn't bother with this card.

LOD-069 Otohime
Reviewed by: NickWhiz1

Uhhh, I don't get this monster. Seriously. Horrible stats, and a very mediocre Effect. Use Bite Shoes instead =P

LOD-069 Otohime
Reviewed by: Raymond Purnama (a.k.a. TwInSeN21)

This spirit's Effect can be decent if you combo it with Ultimate Offering. Most big attackers have one slight weakness; they have low defense. Summoned Skull, Fiend Megacyber, Jinzo, Goblin Attack Force, Gemini Elf all have less than 1500 DEF. Just use Ultimate Offering to summon two Monsters (one being Otohime) and you can easily get rid of your opponent's big hitters by switching them to DEF before you attack.

LOD-070 Hino-Kagu-Tsuchi
Reviewed by: NickWhiz1

More useful than Yamata Dragon. You may sacrifice field advantage, but your opponent loses any hand advantage they get, because, well, they won't have a hand left =/ I would be cautious with this card, because although it's very risky, it can be devastating.

LOD-070 Hino-Kagu-Tsuchi
Reviewed by: Raymond Purnama (a.k.a. TwInSeN21)

This card is almost the same as Yamata Dragon, but it discards your opponent's hand instead. The problem is, in the mid-game, your opponent would only have 0-3 cards on average. It's not worth the trouble when you can easily discard your opponent's hand via Robbin' Goblin, White Magical Hat, Delinquent Duo, The Forceful Sentry, Confiscation, etc…

LOD-071 Asura Priest
Reviewed by: NickWhiz1

The ultimate Scapegoat killer (Spear Dragon places second =/). If you dare put an Axe of Despair or United We Stand on this monster, your opponent's monsters are completely screwed. However, I much prefer Raigeki, Dark Hole, Torrential Tribute, and Mirror Force to destroy my opponent's monsters. Works well in a Spirit/Light deck, though.

LOD-071 Asura Priest
Reviewed by: Raymond Purnama (a.k.a. TwInSeN21)

This card has only one purpose: to clear your opponent's field of monsters. Simply attach a power up like Axe of Despair and you are virtually guaranteed to clear your opponent's monsters. It's great against Scapegoat Tokens (imagine attacking four Goat Tokens while you have a Fairy Meteor Crush on Asura Priest!) and monsters like Mystic Tomato and Nimble Momonga. It is one of the most underrated cards of all time.

LOD-072 Fushi No Tori
Reviewed by: NickWhiz1

You'll rarely ever get a direct attack with this monster, so it's not worth it. There are better LP recovery cards in the game, plus it's level four, so it doesn't help Fire Princess one bit :/

LOD-072 Fushi No Tori
Reviewed by: Raymond Purnama (a.k.a. TwInSeN21)

This card is decent, but there's no point in gaining life unless you run a Fire Princess deck. Unfortunately you don't want to run it in a Fire Princess deck as well. Life Gaining might be fun, but is not really needed in most decks.

LOD-073 Super Robolady
Reviewed by: NickWhiz1

One of the most mediocre Fusions in the game. Seriously, it is.

LOD-073 Super Robolady
Reviewed by: Raymond Purnama (a.k.a. TwInSeN21)

A sorry excuse for a Fusion. There is no reason why you would want to play this card. The Fusion materials are awful and unplayable. The switch effect might be nice, but it's pointless. Don't bother with it

LOD-074 Super Roboyarou
Reviewed by: NickWhiz1

Like his "sister", one of the most mediocre Fusions in the game. Plus, I think one of them is typo'd compared to the Japanese version. I forget which one, though.

LOD-074 Super Roboyarou
Reviewed by: Raymond Purnama (a.k.a. TwInSeN21)

Again, another sorry excuse for a Fusion. There is no reason why you would want to play this card. The Fusion materials are plain awful and unplayable. The switch effect might be nice but it's pointless. Don't bother with it.

LOD-075 Fengsheng Mirror
Reviewed by: NickWhiz1

Ehhh…no. On average, your opponent will only play one Spirit monster (gee, I wonder what THAT could be), and the Hand Disruption Trio (Confiscation, Delinquent Duo, and The Forceful Sentry) do a much more efficient job of getting rid of it. Don't even bother Side Decking it unless your metagame is full of Spirit decks.

LOD-075 Fengsheng Mirror
Reviewed by: Raymond Purnama (a.k.a. TwInSeN21)

I would use this in a Sidedeck in case you run into someone who plays a Spirit Deck. If you just want to use it to get rid of the annoying Yata-Garasu, just use something like Confiscation as it is more playable.

LOD-076 Spring of Rebirth
Reviewed by: SomeGuy.

The only deck I see this working in is Exodia with an army of Penguin Soldier. Even then it wouldn't be very good. It could be combined with Fire Princess, but it isn't likely to happen.

LOD-076 Spring of Rebirth
Reviewed by: Raymond Purnama (a.k.a. TwInSeN21)

I could only see this card being played in a Fire Princess deck. Once you lock your opponent, simply summon a Spirit Monster over and over again to deal damage to your opponent.

LOD-077 Heart of Clear Water
Reviewed by: SomeGuy.

Heart of Clear Water is a great addition to Clown Control. It's as if it was made for it. Besides White Magical Hat, Dream Clown, and Marauding Captain, Heart of Clear Water doesn't have other good uses. It has a very specific function.

LOD-077 Heart of Clear Water
Reviewed by: Raymond Purnama (a.k.a. TwInSeN21)

If you want a good defense, all you need to do is equip this to something like a Scapegoat Token. Watch out for Monsters with Fairy Meteor Crush effect (a.k.a. Trample in Magic: The Gathering) though.

LOD-078 A Legendary Ocean
Reviewed by: SomeGuy.

The obvious use for this card is in a Water deck based around The Legendary Fisherman. It's not very good in other deck types. However, it does its job well in a solid Water deck.

🔯🔯🔯

LOD-078 A Legendary Ocean
Reviewed by: Raymond Purnama (a.k.a. TwInSeN21)

This field card is a MUST if you are playing a Legendary Fisherman deck. Legendary Fisherman becomes a non Tribute Monster, Suijin becomes only a one Tribute Monster, while 7 Colored Fish and Giant Red Seasnake can attack even if Gravity Bind is out. Not to mention the obvious combo with Tornado Wall that could protect your LP forever…

🔯🔯🔯🔯🔯

LOD-079 Fusion Sword Murasame Blade
Reviewed by: SomeGuy.

This card isn't bad for a straight Warrior deck. The secondary effect of it not being able to be destroyed by cards that destroy Magic cards is what makes it decent. Although, it isn't a must-have for most Warrior decks.

🔯🔯

LOD-079 Fusion Sword Murasame Blade
Reviewed by: Raymond Purnama (a.k.a. TwInSeN21)

This card is an excellent power up for Warrior decks. One of the main problems with Power Ups is that they can easily be destroyed by M/T Removal, especially Mystical Space Typhoon during battle phase. An 800 increase in attack or something like Freed the Matchless General makes it big enough to handle most monsters your opponent has in his or her arsenal. However, relying too much on Power Ups can be dangerous.

🔯🔯🔯

LOD-080 Smoke Grenade of the Thief
Reviewed by: SomeGuy.

Smoke Grenade of the Thief is one of those cards that seems decent, but really isn't. There are so many ways around this card it isn't even funny. Stick to your Confiscation, The Forceful Sentry, and Delinquent Duo.

🔯🔯

LOD-080 Smoke Grenade of the Thief
Reviewed by: Raymond Purnama (a.k.a. TwInSeN21)

If you have this card out, your opponent might think twice before using his Heavy Storm or Harpie's Feather Duster. However, if your opponent gets rid of the monster it was equipped to, you would not be able to use the Effect, making it less playable. It's an okay card.

🔯🔯

LOD-081 Creature Swap
Reviewed by: SomeGuy.

Creature Swap is a solid card that combos well with Sinister Serpent, Witch of the Black Forest, Sangan, and even Scapegoat. As you can see, there are many ways around its drawbacks. When used correctly, it can be devastating for your opponent.

🔯🔯🔯🔯

LOD-081 Creature Swap
Reviewed by: Raymond Purnama (a.k.a. TwInSeN21)

Ah, how I love this card! There are a lot of combos that come to my mind when I think about using this card. Simply summon something weak in attack mode and use Creature Swap. If you give him something like Witch/Sangan/Nimble/Mystic Tomato, you will still get their Effects and not your opponent. If you use it with a Spirit Monster, the Spirit Monster will simply return to your hand at the end of the turn. Creature Swap becomes a permanent Change of Heart. Be careful if your opponent has multiple monsters out. It's best to use Creature Swap when your opponent only has one monster on the field.

🔯🔯🔯🔯🔯

LOD-082 Spiritual Energy Settle Machine
Reviewed by: SomeGuy.

The End Phase cost of this card is too high to make it playable. Add in the fact that all your opponent has to do to clear the field is destroy Spiritual Energy Settle Machine, and it becomes as bad as Toon World.

LOD-082 Spiritual Energy Settle Machine
Reviewed by: Raymond Purnama (a.k.a. TwInSeN21)

You would only play this card if you run a lot of Spirit Monsters, especially if you plan on playing Spirit Monsters that require tributes. As for the cost of maintaining this card, you probably want Sinister Serpent as it will always return to your hand. In a way, this is the Toon World for Spirit Monsters.

LOD-083 Second Coin Toss
Reviewed by: SomeGuy.

The only use for this card is in a casual Coin Flip deck. One of my friends made a hilarious version of the deck that is fun to play. Tournament wise, this is just another unplayable card from LOD.

LOD-083 Second Coin Toss
Reviewed by: Raymond Purnama (a.k.a. TwInSeN21)

Don't like the result of that Gamble? Barrel Dragon? Jirai Gumo? or Time Wizard? That's why this card was printed. If you like to play cards that rely on coin flips, just play this card as it improves your odds by 50%.

LOD-084 Convulsion of Nature
Reviewed by: SomeGuy.

Convulsion of Nature is a stupid, pointless card. Any combos that result from it are not very good. The tiny advantage it gives isn't really worth it. Especially since your opponent gets the exact same advantage.

LOD-084 Convulsion of Nature
Reviewed by: Raymond Purnama (a.k.a. TwInSeN21)

This is an interesting card. There might some combo it will work with in the future, but right now it's just like a Respect Play. Most decks don't need it.

LOD-085 The Secret of the Bandit
Reviewed by: SomeGuy.

This card can be good in a Hand Disruption deck. The fact that it doesn't get screwed over by Mystical Space Typhoon, Heavy Storm, Harpie's Feather Duster, and Jinzo like Robbin' Goblin makes it fairly decent. Although, it has its own share of disadvantages.

LOD-085 The Secret of The Bandit
Reviewed by: Raymond Purnama (a.k.a. TwInSeN21)

This card is best used on Hayabusa Knight and Asura Priest. With the right setup, your opponent can lose his entire hand in one turn. You can win by the Yata-Lock or by card advantage.

LOD-086 After Genocide
Reviewed by: SomeGuy.

This card provides a mediocre way to clear the field when all you are stuck with is weak monsters. The problem with this strategy is that most good decks won't, or shouldn't, have many weak Monsters in the first place.

LOD-086 After Genocide
Reviewed by: Raymond Purnama (a.k.a. TwInSeN21)

This card is used when you are really desperate. If your opponent has a massive army out and you know you can't beat them, you can use something like Asura Priest and attack all of your opponent's monsters. The result? You lose one Asura Priest (and some LP) while your opponent loses all of his or her Monsters. It's not too shabby, but very situational so not really useful as well.

LOD-087 Magic Reflector
Reviewed by: SomeGuy.

The best use for this card is in Stall, Exodia, and possibly Legendary Fishermen decks. Stall and Exodia decks will be able to better protect their Messenger of Peace, while Legendary Fishermen decks can salvage their A Legendary Ocean.

LOD-087 Magic Reflector
Reviewed by: Raymond Purnama (a.k.a. TwInSeN21)

If you really want to save that Messenger of Peace/Snatch Steal/A Legendary Ocean, you might want to consider playing this card. If there is a Permanent Magic card/Equip that you must protect, this is the card for you.

LOD-088 Blast with Chain
Reviewed by: SomeGuy.

Blast with Chain isn't too bad for a Trap card. It's not tournament playable because it's a Trap card, and there are many ways around its Secondary Effect. Although the recoil that Blast with Chain gives to your opponent can be pretty solid.

LOD-088 Blast With Chain
Reviewed by: Raymond Purnama (a.k.a. TwInSeN21)

This card is surprisingly good. It's like what Reinforcement wants to be. Being a Trap card makes it unpredictable and might cause your opponent to suicide his monster. After that, if your opponent destroys it by an Effect (or you can do it yourself), you can destroy any card on the field, including monster cards. Now that's a nice after effect!

LOD-089 Disappear
Reviewed by: SomeGuy.

Disappear is one of those cards that gives you no card advantage whatsoever. Its Petite Effect hardly impacts anything besides Skull Lair and Bazoo the Soul-Eater. The Effect of Fiber Jar has already penalized both of those cards.

LOD-089 Disappear
Reviewed by: Raymond Purnama (a.k.a. TwInSeN21)

Soul Release is better in most cases since you remove more cards and you can use it straight away. Disappear is better when your opponent tries to use something like Monster Reborn/Call of the Haunted/Premature Burial. Once they select the monster that they want to Reborn, activate Disappear to "negate" the effect. It's not too bad.

LOD-090 Bubble Crash
Reviewed by: SomeGuy.

Bubble Crash has the most devastating effect against Control decks, namely Exodia. If used at the right time against an Exodia deck, you can potentially destroy four to five cards. That's good card advantage. However, Bubble Crash is a very situational card. Given that fact, its rating drops immensely.

LOD-090 Bubble Crash
Reviewed by: Raymond Purnama (a.k.a. TwInSeN21)

This card is so situational that it won't be used often. If your opponent relies on cards like Cyber Jar and Morphing Jar to gain a lot of cards, you can use this card to counter them. Make sure you time it right or you might lose a lot of cards in the process.

LOD-091 Royal Oppression
Reviewed by: SomeGuy.

This is one of those cards that sit in your Side Deck until the right match shows up. It's definitely not a card to use in your Main Deck. You also have to make sure it won't backfire against your deck.

LOD-091 Royal Oppression
Reviewed by: Raymond Purnama (a.k.a. TwInSeN21)

An interesting card. It's too bad your opponent gets to use the Effect as well. You might want to Sidedeck it against someone who relies on Special Summonings.

LOD-092 Bottomless Trap Hole
Reviewed by: SomeGuy.

Bottomless Trap Hole is solid Monster Removal that's best suited for the Side Deck. It can be decent in the Main Deck. The fact that it removes the monster from the game and hits Special Summons is what gives Bottomless Trap Hole its edge.

LOD-092 Bottomless Trap Hole
Reviewed by: Raymond Purnama (a.k.a. TwInSeN21)

Since this card has been ruled that it can get rid of multiple targets after a Cyber Jar, the combo is pretty good. Since it also can get rid of Special Summon monsters (other than Jinzo) a lot of people consider it better than Trap Hole. I still prefer Torrential Tribute.

LOD-093 Bad Reaction to Simochi
Reviewed by: SomeGuy.

The only decent card that I see this working with is Upstart Goblin. Since Upstart Goblin is restricted to one, it's not even worth attempting.

LOD-093 Bad Reaction to Simochi
Reviewed by: Raymond Purnama (a.k.a. TwInSeN21)

Ah, combos. It works well with Snatch Steal. You can combo it with cards like Rain of Mercy. Unless you get this card out though, Rain of Mercy is useless.

LOD-094 Ominous Fortunetelling
Reviewed by: SomeGuy.

Although it can potentially provide 700 free Life Point damage per turn, its randomness is too great. The chance that you're going to name the card correctly, along with the chance of it lasting on the field, outweighs its good points.

LOD-094 Ominous Fortunetelling
Reviewed by: Raymond Purnama (a.k.a. TwInSeN21)

A decent burner card. Since there is no cost to keep it up, you can play as many as you want and wait out your opponent. If he plays most of his cards, you can guess correctly most of the time. If he plays everything down, you won't get to do damage. However, a simple Dark Hole and Heavy Storm and your opponent will be defenseless. If he doesn't play down too many cards, you have fewer threats to deal with on the field. It works either way.

LOD-095 Spirit's Invitation
Reviewed by: SomeGuy.

This card isn't playable because you're bouncing a monster to your opponent's hand at the end of your turn. This Effect adds up to nothing because he or she can just re-summon on their upcoming Main Phase. Most Spirits aren't worth using.

LOD-095 Spirit's Invitation
Reviewed by: Raymond Purnama (a.k.a. TwInSeN21)

Again, another card for Spirit decks. It's not even important, unless you want to use a 3-4 card combo. This card is just not worth it.

LOD-096 Nutrient Z
Reviewed by: SomeGuy.

Nutrient Z may seem pretty good, but it isn't. Both Scapegoat and Waboku are more versatile for stalling. If pressed, Nutrient Z may have some use in a casual Life Gain deck.

LOD-096 Nutrient Z
Reviewed by: Raymond Purnama (a.k.a. TwInSeN21)

It's a decent card, but I'd rather play something like a Waboku. Preventing all damage is better if your opponent has a lot of monsters on the field.

LOD-097 Drop Off
Reviewed by: SomeGuy.

Drop is an arguably better version of Time Seal. They both have their advantages and disadvantages. Since there are so many different scenarios, there's no way one is clearly seen to be better than the other.

LOD-097 Drop Off
Reviewed by: Raymond Purnama (a.k.a. TwInSeN21)

A good disruption to use, especially if you are trying to Yata-Lock your opponent as soon as possible. It might backfire, as your opponent can just Reborn the Monster if you discard one.

LOD-098 Fiend Comedian
Reviewed by: SomeGuy.

This card is too risky to consider using. I wouldn't even use this card with Second Coin Toss. Yes, it's that risky. Call it wrong and you'll be in pain.

LOD-098 Fiend Comedian
Reviewed by: Raymond Purnama (a.k.a. TwInSeN21)

Ah, another card that relies on Coin Flips. This is another reason to use Second Coin Toss. If you really want to remove your opponent's graveyard, you should just use Soul Release. It's guaranteed to remove any five cards of your choice. Calling it Tails can be either good or bad in this case. In a way, it thins your deck and you get to power up Bazoo and Skull Lair. I heard there was some deadly combo in Japan involving this card. We'll have to wait and see…

LOD-099 Last Turn
Reviewed by: SomeGuy.

The only good aspect to Last Turn is there are a few ways to auto-win. The easiest consists of using Last Turn and Jowgen the Spiritualist. However, don't expect to attain 1000 or less Life Points easily. Last Turn decks definitely require plenty of setup to be successful.

LOD-099 Last Turn
Reviewed by: Raymond Purnama (a.k.a. TwInSeN21)

An alternative way to win if you rely on cards that cost LP (Toons, Solemn Judgment and the soon to be released Cyber-Stein). A bit too unreliable in most decks, especially since you can only have two copies of it in your deck.

LOD-100 Injection Fairy Lily
Reviewed by: SomeGuy.

Injection Fairy Lily is an extremely destructive monster. Not only does it pack a huge punch, but it's versatile at doing so. Make sure to use the Effect at the proper time. I've seen less experienced players lose to bad judgment. Use it correctly and it will win you many games.

LOD-100 Injection Fairy Lily
Reviewed by: Raymond Purnama (a.k.a. TwInSeN21)

Once you get her out, it's seldom that your opponent can get rid of her through battle (assuming you have the LP to pay). You can fetch her with both Witch and Sangan. You could also Special Summon her out with Giant Rat if you want. If you really want a BIG beatstick, play her.

Top Ten

CREATURE CARDS

Yu-Gi-Oh! Legacy of Darkness released some brutal creatures with huge Effects, rather than your standard Traps and Magic. Now, on to the top 10!

By Chris Schroeder

1. Yata-Garasu - LOD - 000

Yata-Garasu is number one in Legacy of Darkness and with a big reason. This creature is a game winner and all around just broken (broken means very, very good and should be banned). Its Effect makes your opponent skip his draw phase when it does damage to his or her life points. Its Effect can easily lock your opponent and you can just keep on attacking for 200 each turn. Once your opponent is down to about 1000-2000 life points, then you can monster reborn or just simply summon a monster to take out the last of their life points. There's nothing your opponent can do to stop it unless he or she can destroy the bird or make you discard it from your hand. Bird decks are now running rampant. You'll want to include cards that can destroy it or you might find yourself in the Bird Lock deck. The best defense against Yata-Garasu is Sinister Serpent.

2. Exiled Force - LOD-023

Number two on the list is Exiled Force. A creature that has the Flip Effect of Man-Eater Bug but just the Effect. When this monster is on the field face-up, you may destroy this creature to destroy one of your opponent's monsters face down or face up. You can easily clear the field and open your opponent for direct damage. Or, you just clear the way for Yata-Garasu, which is what this card is usually used to do. I've seen tons of decks run two or three of these. They are very effective in any deck. With this card being able to still use its Effect before it is trap holed, it makes it one of the greatest Effect monsters in the game.

3. Fairy Injection Lily - LOD-100

The Lily is a personal favorite of mine. Sure it's a small creature. Its Effect gives it a huge punch. I do mean huge. For the cost 2000 life points, you may increase her attack power by 3000 making her a 3400 creature. That's big enough to take out Jinzo, Blue Eyes White Dragon, Goblin Attack Force, etc. Upper Deck has ruled it that way. It makes her a very powerful creature. Though it will be limit one soon. It is one card that I always like to run, since it can take out those overly used cards. Her price is pretty steep but she gets the job done.

4. Marauding Captain - LOD-018

The captain is number four on the top ten list. His Effect allows you to special summon a level four or lower creature from your hand onto the field. This is great in beat down since you play with all the best level four creatures. Also, it works well in a Hand Destruction deck. You can summon him and if it looks safe, you can summon White Magical Hat and start discarding cards from your opponent's hand. Its other Effect says your opponent may not attack another Warrior type monster on the field as long as this card is face up on the field. If you have two of these out, they protect each other and your opponent can't attack them. This creature is great in an all Warrior deck as well.

5. Spear Dragon - LOD-035

A Level Four 1900 attack monster with a built in Fairy Meteor Crush. Just amazing. Spear Dragon is number five on the list since it's one of the most effective level four monsters in Beatdown decks. Its Effect is if this card attacks with an ATK that is higher than the DEF of your opponent's Defense Position monster, the difference is inflicted as Battle Damage to your opponent's life points. When this card

attacks, it is changed to Defense Position at the end of the Damage Step. Its main enemy is itself since it has 0 defense leaving you open to an attack of 1900 from another Spear Dragon.

However, with the right protection it shouldn't be a big problem. This is an all around great Beatdown monster. It's effective since defense mode doesn't help your opponent when this monster is on the field and the life points go down fast. It's also great against Goblin Attack Force since GAF stays in defense mode longer than this card does. It's very powerful.

6. Fiber Jar - LOD-056

A new jar from Legacy of Darkness. Fiber Jar makes number six on the list. It has an Effect that can be pretty annoying. When this creature is flipped over, the game resets. You shuffle your

hand, all cards on the field, and your discard pile back into your deck and draw five cards. It can be a game winner if you are able to flip this card over during your turn. It clears the field, gives you a

new hand, and your opponent doesn't have a chance to stop anything. This can also shuffle back Yata-Garasu if it got discarded. Fiber Jar has plenty of uses and it has its place as a game winner if played right. Watch out for this card!

7. Twin Headed Behemoth - LOD-063

Two monsters in one. Twin Headed Behemoth makes number seven with its once per game Effect. When this card is destroyed, it returns to the field at the end of the turn as a special summon with 1000 attack

and DEF. I've seen this card work very effectively with Hand Manipulation decks. With Robbin Goblin in play, you try to attack with this monster. If not, you get a second chance and its special summoned the second time to get a card from their hand. It has a rather small attack power of 1500, but its effect is what makes it playable. It's two monsters in one and having monsters on the field is always great.

8. Dark Ruler Ha Des - LOD-001

Dark Ruler Ha Des is number eight on the list. It can be labeled as the Effect killer. While this monster is face up on the field, it negates the Effects of Effect monsters that your Fiend type

monsters destroy as a result of battle. This is a nice Effect. It can negate Witch of the Black Forest, Sangan, Magician of Faith, Cyber Jar, etc. if your Fiend type monsters destroy them. It has an attack power of 2450 which can take out pesky Jinzo. It's a level six monster that can't be special summoned from the graveyard. However, Fiend decks can get brutal with Ha Des on the field. A nice addition to Fiend Decks and it only needs one tribute.

9. Airknight Parshath - LOD-062

A level five monster that has a Meteor Crush Effect. You get to draw a card and it has an attack power of 1900. This is pretty nice for a level five monster. It gives you an easy chance to draw a card. For a tribute, this is not as bad as most people think. This is more suited for a Light theme type deck. You could toss it in a Beatdown deck, but it will probably slow down the deck. The problem is you need a monster on the field to tribute summon for it.

You are better off with Spear Dragon. It has the same effects except for the "Draw a card". This monster gets to take number nine on the list. It has Nice effects, but are a bit costly.

10. Asura Priest - LOD-071

The final creature of the top ten. Asura Priest is another one of those Spirit cards that goes back to your hand at the end of the turn. It has an attack power of 1700, it's a level four and it has a very nice Effect. This card can attack all monsters on your opponent's side of the field. You cannot attack your opponent directly if you attack any monsters first. This works well against face down monsters, Scapegoats, or even monsters in attack mode. The right kind of field magic can boost it up, and it can attack and take out a field of level four monsters easy. Also, it can still attack your opponent directly if it didn't attack any monsters.

■

Top Ten
magic and trap

By Ken Jackson

Legacy of Darkness brought about major boosts to Fiend, Warrior, and Dragon decks, but what cards are there that can help ANY deck? Lets take a look at some of the best Magic and Trap cards in the set and see what niches they can fill in the current environment, whether it be deck type specific, or all around helpful.

Bottomless Trap Hole LOD-092

When your opponent Normal Summons, Flip Summons, or Special Summons a monster with an ATK of 1500 or more, the monster is destroyed and removed from play.

A very good all around card. Especially since it not only destroys the monster, but removes it from play as well. Any monsters that get their effect by going to the Graveyard don't get it with Bottomless Trap Hole. Another great advantage to this is that it can also hit Special Summons as well. No more discarding than Monster Reborning their big two tribute monsters, Bottomless Trap Hole takes care of that very nicely.

The one downside to this is that it has upped the target's attack by 500 points over Trap Hole, so it's ineffective against a lot of the troublesome smaller cards like Witch, Sangan, Exiled Force and Marauding Captain. Still, it is a very solid card and if you are still using Trap Hole, you should look at replacing at least one or two with this pumped up variant.

👁 🜏 🜏 🜏

The A Forces LOD-027

For every face-up Warrior-Type and Spellcaster-Type monster on your side of the field, increase the ATK of all Warrior-Type monsters on your side of the field by 200 points.

This is a very powerful card, undoubtedly one that should be in EVERY Warrior deck. Very simply, it increases all your Warriors. Fast. If you have one Warrior out, it's increased by 200. If you have two out, each of them are increased by 400 points. If you have two Warriors and two A. Forces, they are each increased by 800 points… see where I'm going with this?

A. Forces makes the Warrior deck very deadly, and since it's not an Equip Magic Card, it can't be taken care of as easily as destroying the attached monster.

👁 🜏 🜏 🜏 👁

Fiend Comedian LOD-098

Toss a coin and call it. If you call it right, all your opponent's cards in the Graveyard are removed from play immediately. If you call it wrong, send a number of cards equal to the cards in your opponent's Graveyard from your Deck to your Graveyard.

Perhaps one of the most underrated cards in the set, Fiend Comedian has the power to have decks built around it, as well as the power to stop cards such as Bazoo and Skull Lair.

The premise is simple. Once your opponent declares that they are going to use Skull Lair or Bazoo's effect, activate Fiend Comedian. Since chains resolve backwards, Fiend Comedian is resolved first. Pick your side, flip the coin, and with any luck, you'll remove their entire Graveyard from play before they have the chance to make Bazoo more powerful than he deserves.

The downside of course is that if you guess wrong, you have to discard cards from your deck equal to the number in your opponent's grave. Not a pretty site when you have to discard 20 cards of your own… But still, if you play your cards right, and play Fiend Comedian with Second Coin Toss, your odds of that happening are greatly reduced.

🜏 🜏 🜏

Bad Reaction to Simochi LOD-093

As long as this card remains face-up on the field, the effect of increasing your opponent's Life Points is negated and changed to inflict the same amount of points in Direct Damage to your opponent's Life Points.

Well, I'm not sure what Simochi is, but if the card's effect is any indication, Simochi is gaining life points, thus a bad reaction to it would be the loss of life, right?

This card is one of the main reasons Upstart Goblin is limited to one. (That and

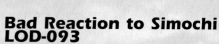

he fact that almost ANY card that lets you draw more cards is limited to one…) With Simochi out, not only do you get to draw a card, but your opponent also takes 1000 direct damage. Cards like Nimble Momonga and Enchanted Javelin now become less annoying with this card… and hey, if your opponent is going to be losing 1000 life each time you destroy a Momonga, they might think twice about bringing out the other two right away.

Bubble Crash LOD-090

This card can only be activated when any player has more than 6 cards on the field and/or in their hand. The player(s) must then select and send cards to their respective Graveyards until the amount remaining on the field and their hand is 5.

This is a very entertaining card, as its fun to watch your opponent try and figure out which of their well thought out hand and field are going to have to be limited. Best played when your opponent has a full hand and very full field and you have barely anything out.

It's interesting to see what people get rid of too. Sometimes they will get rid of monsters from the field, or equip magic cards also seem to be a favorite too. Just remember that Bubble Crash's effect also goes double for you, so don't be playing it when its going to hurt you just as much as your opponent.

Ominous Fortunetelling LOD-094

During your Standby Phase, select 1 card randomly from your opponent's hand and call the Type of card (Monster, Magic, or Trap). If you call it right, inflict 700 points of Direct Damage to your opponent's Life Points. You can use this effect only once per turn.

Pick a card, any card. If you guess right, your opponent eats 700 damage. If you guess wrong… well, nothing.

This is another fun card, and it comes in very handy when your opponent has only a couple cards in their hand. Very effective against Spirit decks since you always know that the Spirit monster is going to end up in their hand by the time you get to use this.

If you find yourself constantly being hit with Ominous Fortunetelling and can't figure out why they can keep guessing, make

sure to shuffle your hand while you're playing… and don't always put Yata back in the same spot. That's what they'll be watching for.

Fusion Sword Murasame Blade LOD-079

This card can only be equipped to Warrior-Type monsters. A monster equipped with this card increases its ATK by 800 points. This card cannot be destroyed by effects that destroy Magic Cards.

Think of it as a mini Axe of Despair that can't be destroyed. Put this on any warrior (my favorite is Hayabusa Knight) and it instantly becomes +800 until its destroyed. Heavy Storm, Harpy's Feather Duster, Mystical Space Typhoon… none of these can get rid of the mighty Murasame Blade.

The only way to effectively get rid of it is by negating it with Imperial Order, or destroying the monster that it's equipped to. Not always an easy task if you have to attack a Marauding Captain equipped with one of these and there's an A. Forces or two around as well.

Reinforcement of the Army LOD-028

Move 1 Level 4 or lower Warrior-Type monster from your Deck to your hand. Your Deck is then shuffled.

Very simple card, with a simple goal. Take one low level warrior from your deck and put it in your hand. Very effective if you are about to play the Marauding Captain, so that you can ensure to not let its Special Summon effect go to waste. Also great for grabbing that Exiled Force to take care of something that's pestering you, like a Jinzo, or Spear Cretin wall.

A Legendary Ocean LOD-078

This card's name is treated as "Umi". Downgrade all WATER monsters in both player's hands and on the field by 1 Level. Increases the ATK and DEF of all WATER monsters by 200 points.

Think of this as an Umi on Simochi… whatever Simochi may be. Legendary Ocean is the pumped up version of Umi that not only increases all ATK and DEF of

Water monsters by 200, it also decreases their level.

Think of a Level 3 Seven Colored Fish with 2000 ATK that can get past Gravity Bind. how about a no tribute Legendary Fisherman, still with its great effect. All of this and more can be achieved with a Legendary Ocean.

One small note though. Remember that you can only have 3 of these OR 3 Umi's in your deck, since Legendary Ocean counts as Umi. Of course, with Legendary Ocean out, why would you WANT Umi still?

Creature Swap Normal Magic LOD-081

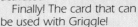

Both players select 1 monster on their respective fields and switch control of them to each other. The battle positions of these cards cannot change during the turn this card is activated

Finally! The card that can be used with Griggle! Creature Swap is like a double-sided change of heart that lasts until the monsters are destroyed. Kinda. True, you get to keep the monster that your opponent gives you, but unlike Change of Heart of Snatch Steal, you have no control over what monster you're getting.

This is defiantly best used when your opponent only has one monster, and you have something weaker that you can easily destroy. Also, a very devious way to play this is to give your opponent a Spirit Monster, and then take their Jinzo or other powerful monster. The Spirit goes back to your hand at the end of your turn, and they're left with nothing but an open field.

So there are 10 of the best Magic and Trap cards in the set, but they are by no means the ONLY good cards in the set. There are a lot of cards that benefit Dragons, and even more that help out the Warrior Decks. As we continue to get new expansions, the legitimacy of 'typed' decks is growing stronger. Legacy of Darkness focused on Dragons and Warriors, with some small help to fiends. Pharaohic Guardian will give the same kind of treatment to others. The days of generic beatdowns with any kind of monsters is coming to an end… the question is, what type of deck are you going to play? Generic beatdowns with any kind of monsters is coming to an end… the question is, what type of deck are you going to play? ■

Killer Deck

STRUGGLES OF Chaos

By Nick Moore, a.k.a. NickWhiz1

After doing two straight Beatdown decks in the last couple of books, I figured I'd use something different. I decided to build a deck based around one of the three sub-types boosted by the Legacy of Darkness set -- Warriors.

This is the first set where Warriors truly become a viable archetype. It will continue to get more powerful as we get further into the game.

If anyone is wondering about the name, the Japanese set where the Warriors began its reign was Struggle of Chaos (it's also the first half of the English LOD set, coincidence?).

This deck may take a slightly different approach than other Warrior decks. You'll see.

Monsters:

Exiled Force - Everything that Man-Eater Bug wanted to be, and more. It has better stats, its Effect is not a flip, and it effectively makes recursion cards double as monster removal. It also works well in almost every deck.

Fiber Jar - The almighty reset button, and a pretty spiffy picture to boot. I mean, it's a tree rocket. What's not to like about it? Flip it over, and reswarm on an empty field.

Goblin Attack Force - Currently the strongest Level four monster. How can you argue with 2300 ATK? =/

Injection Fairy Lily - Lily can pass for a Warrior, can't she? Of course, no Warrior can pump itself up to 3400 like Lily, so I guess we can make an exception.

Jinzo - Jinzo can pass for a Warrior, can't it? Well, it looks like a Warrior, but no Warrior can negate all Traps and get away with 2400 attack for level six, so we need to make another exception.

Marauding Captain - This guy has been popping up in non-Warrior decks because it can aid in mass swarming. I guess it would fit in a Warrior deck too, right?

Morphing Jar - Don't throw stuff at me if you don't have one of these. It can easily be replaced or removed, but it helps replenish your hand after using Marauding Captain. If you have it, good. If you don't, just ignore it =/

Sangan - You have to like this little critter. He can search out everything in this deck except the heavy hitters (Goblin, Spear, Jinzo), including Marauding Captain and Exiled Force.

Sinister Serpent - Graceful Charity? Get this back. Morphing Jar? Get this back. Painful Choice? Get this back. Opposing Delinquent Duo? Get this back. Should I continue? Get th……no.

Witch of the Black Forest - The best monster in the game, PERIOD. End of sentence. Look at your restriction list. What's common between all the monsters? Oh, they all have 1500 or less Defense? K, just making sure.

Yata-Garasu - People say this is the best monster in the game, and they have a convincing argument. One of the few cards that creates a perfect (note - very perfect) lock.

Why no Freed the Matchless General? - Frankly, Freed is a little slow. Yes, its Effects are nice, but it can't be searched out, and a Goblin can suicide and kill it. Besides, Reinforcement of the Army does the job better, and it doesn't sacrifice your draw phase.

Magic:

Change of Heart - Sure, I'll swipe your big, bad Jinzo and hit you with it for 2400, then sacrifice it for MY Jinzo!

Confiscation - While it is expensive, it can eliminate potential threats like Yata-Garasu. Also, you can see what your opponent is planning for you.

Dark Hole - While not as versatile as Raigeki, it has its uses, particularly with Witch and Sangan.

Delinquent Duo - This card nets you instant hand advantage (or at least close to it) at the cost of 1000 Life Points. An excellent early-game play (try 1st turn!)

Graceful Charity - While it doesn't give you card advantage (it's basically trading 3 cards for 3 cards), it does thin out your deck and gives you quick access to that Raigeki or Harpie's Feather Duster you need to finish off your opponent.

Harpie's Feather Duster - The Magic/Trap version of Raigeki. It's easier to find, because you can get Worldwide Edition like, everywhere =/

Heavy Storm - The Magic/Trap version of Dark Hole. It's still useful, despite the advent of Harpie's Feather Duster and Mystical Space Typhoon. Use it wisely =/

Monster Reborn – We have another abuseable card. Bring back Witch/Sangan for another round of searching, bring back Exiled Force for another round of destruction, or bring back Jinzo for another round of Trap negation.

Mystical Space Typhoon - Not playing three of these is like eating pizza without cheese. You can do it, but why?

Nobleman of Crossout - Although players have lowered the number of Flip Effect monsters in their decks, there's still a couple out there that are dangerous. Use this to get them, and get them good.

Painful Choice - You can give your opponent one of these when you use this card. Try picking five cards that will give you an advantage, but won't hurt you if they go to the Graveyard. Also, it works well for discarding useless cards later in the game.

Pot of Greed - Bill. That's all I have to say.

Monsters: (15)
3x Goblin Attack Force (PSV-094)
2x Marauding Captain (LOD-018)
1x Exiled Force (LOD-023)
1x Fiber Jar (LOD-056)
1x Injection Fairy Lily (LOD-100)
1x Jinzo (PSV-000)
1x Morphing Jar (TP2-001)
1x Sangan (MRD-069/SDJ-019)
1x Sinister Serpent (SDD-002)
1x Spear Dragon (LOD-035)
1x Witch of the Black Forest (MRD-116/SDP-014)
1x Yata-Garasu (LOD-000)

Magic: (21)
3x Mystical Space Typhoon (MRL-047/SDP-032)
2x Graceful Charity (SDP-040)
2x Reinforcement of the Army (LOD-023)
1x Change of Heart (MRD-060/SDJ-030/SDP-030/SDY-032)
1x Confiscation (MRL-038)
1x Dark Hole (LOB-052/SDJ-026/SDK-022/SDP-026/SDY-022)
1x Delinquent Duo (MRL-039)
1x Harpie's Feather Duster (SDD-003)
1x Heavy Storm (MRD-142)
1x Monster Reborn (LOB-118/SDJ-035/SDK-036/SDP-035/SDY-030)
1x Nobleman of Crossout (PSV-034)
1x Painful Choice (MRL-049)
1x Pot of Greed (LOB-119/TP3-014)
1x Premature Burial (PSV-037)
1x Raigeki (LOB-053)
1x Snatch Steal (MRL-036)
1x The Forceful Sentry (MRL-045)

Traps: (5)
1x Call of the Haunted (PSV-012)
1x Imperial Order (PSV-104)
1x Magic Cylinder (LON-104)
1x Mirror Force (MRD-138)
1x Waboku (SDJ-046/SDP-044/SDY-040)

Total Cards: 41
Side Deck:
It doesn't make sense to suggest a Side Deck, as the Side Deck depends on your metagame. For matters related to Side Decks, Read the Side Deck article later in the book. It covers everything you need to know.

Premature Burial - The same thing as Monster Reborn, just not as completely broken.

Raigeki - If Pot of Greed didn't exist, this would be the best card in the game. But it does, so you have to settle with destroying all of your opponent's monsters with the second best card in the game =/

Reinforcement of the Army - If you don't want to waste Sangan/Witch of the Black Forest to pull out your Warriors, use this instead. I don't know what Konami was thinking when they made this card =/

Snatch Steal - Yoink. That's all I have to say.

The Forceful Sentry - Kind of like Confiscation, but it doesn't cost anything. However, you still lose the card, and it slightly thickens your opponent's deck. Not bad.

Traps:

Call of the Haunted - Chainable recursion, and you can use it during your opponent's turn!

Imperial Order - What Magic Jammer wants to be when it grows up.

Magic Cylinder - Direct damage and attack negation in one card. Nice.

Mirror Force - It may be old, but it still does the job in a timely fashion.

Waboku - A little added protection in case of severe bum rushes (i.e. swarming).

Conclusion:

I hope you enjoy my look at a Warrior deck. Warriors are my second favorite archetype (behind Zombies, and you'll see why in the future). You can bug me at the usual e-mail address. If not, that's better for both of us. ∎

Killer Deck

CLOWN CONTROL

By Vijay Seixas, a.k.a. SomeGuy

Experienced players who read my last Clown Control article in Pojo's Total Yu-Gi-Oh! Vol. 2 may have noticed that it wasn't awesome for tournament play. At that time, it was directed to the average Yu-Gi-Oh! player who only rarely attends tournaments.

Now with the release of Legacy of Darkness, Clown Control got the necessary boost to make it a solid contender in tournament play. Here's the latest, most competitive version of Clown Control:

In comparison with the last version, the two are completely different decks. This is by far the fastest version of Clown Control. Not only is the latest version faster, but it's also much more stable with the help of Marauding Captain and Heart of Clear Water.

-Monster Cards-

The five new Monsters that were added are Marauding Captain, Injection Fairy Lily, Yata-Garasu, Fiber Jar, and Exiled Force. Four of which are restricted to one which tells you something. Marauding Captain is the primary Dream Clown defender. Not only can he prevent Dream Clown from being attacked, but he is also able to Special Summon Dream Clown the turn he is Regular Summoned.

Injection Fairy Lily is one of the best level three monsters in the entire deck. Its immense strength coupled with excellent versatility gives it the perfect reason to be included in the deck.

Then there's Yata-Garasu. He is an absolute beast. Even if you can't win the game through a Yata-Garasu lock, a few straight attacks from him can give you the card advantage needed to win the game. Never underestimate this card.

Next on the list is Fiber Jar. Not only does Fiber Jar restart an awful game, but it gives you a clear field to attack.

Lastly, there is Exiled Force. Exiled Force is the perfect

answer to any threat. It's very rare
when his Effect cannot destroy a partic-
lar Monster. Exiled Force is great for
etting rid of an opposing Jinzo.

Magic Cards-

Since the last Clown Control version,
few new cards were added as well
s cards that were in the deck long
go. Among the cards that were re-
dded are Confiscation, The Forceful
entry, and Premature Burial. The new
ards include Heart of Clear Water,
einforcement of the Army, and The
Warrior Returning Alive.

Since Yata-Garasu was released, the
ower of Confiscation, The Forceful
entry, and Delinquent Duo doubled.
's the main reason why both The
orceful Sentry and Confiscation were
e-added into Clown Control.
remature Burial also has more uses in
he latest version. I can Premature
urial for Marauding Captain to protect
Dream Clown, or for an Exiled Force
o deal with a threat.

As always, I can Premature Burial for
lost Dream Clown. Heart of Clear
Water is simply the best Equipment
Magic card I could use in this deck. It's
he best protection for any monster,
ut primarily for Dream Clown.

Both Reinforcement of the Army and
The Warrior Returning Alive have many
uses in this latest version. Among the
cards I can search for are Dream
Clown, Marauding Captain, and Exiled
Force. All of which are excellent candi-
dates.

Using The Warrior Returning Alive to
reuse Exiled Force's solid Effect is something that I do often.

-Trap Cards-

If you read the previous version of
Clown Control, you notice the high
amount of Trap cards (10). This was a
big disadvantage against decks that
included Jinzo, which is every tournament deck. I've slimmed it down now
to the bare necessities. Among these
are Gravity Bind, Imperial Order, Mirror
Force, and Magic Cylinder.

You may also have noticed my praise
of Skull Lair in the last article. Skull Lair
still has a very powerful Effect, but it's
now highly countered by Fiber Jar.
Abusing Skull Lair only to have a Fiber
Jar flipped on you can cost you the
game. Even though Dream Clown can
destroy a face-down Fiber Jar, skilled
opponents will always correctly time
their set.

Thus, Skull Lair has been dropped
from the deck. Although,
don't hesitate to run a single
copy in your personal version if you think you can
deal with its disadvantages.
Another great card that was
dropped is Call of the
Haunted. Call of the
Haunted is a very solid card
in the deck, but it wasn't
essential. Unless the Trap
was essential, I wasn't going
to use it.

I am exceptionally happy
with my Trap count at six. It
works like a charm. ∎

(Please keep in mind that
this article was written
before the official release of
restrictions for Legacy of
Darkness. The restrictions
that I'm using came directly
from the Japanese
Restriction List. They will
most likely be the same, or
very near to, the United
States Restriction List when it
is released.)

MYSTICAL SPACE TYPHOON

[MAGIC CARD]

Destroy 1 Magic or Trap Card on the field.

MRL-047
05318639   ©1996 KAZUKI TAKAHASHI

-Monster Cards- 15
3x Dream Clown MRD-080
2x White Magical Hat MRD-016
2x Marauding Captain LOD-018
1x Witch of the Black Forest MRD-116
1x Sangan MRD-069
1x Jinzo PSV-000
1x Sinister Serpent SDD-002
1x Yata-Garasu LOD-000
1x Injection Fairy Lily LOD-100
1x Fiber Jar LOD-056
1x Exiled Force LOD-023

-Magic Cards- 19
3x Mystical Space Typhoon MRL-047
2x Graceful Charity SDP-040
2x Heart of Clear Water LOD-077
1x The Warrior Returning Alive
1x Reinforcement of the Army LOD-028
1x Monster Reborn LOB-118
1x Pot of Greed LOB-119
1x Change of Heart MRD-060
1x Raigeki LOB-053
1x Dark Hole LOB-052
1x Harpie's Feather Duster SDD-003
1x Delinquent Duo MRL-039
1x Confiscation MRL-038
1x The Forceful Sentry MRL-045
1x Premature Burial PSV-037

-Trap Cards- 6
3x Gravity Bind PSV-073
1x Imperial Order PSV-104
1x Mirror Force MRD-138
1x Magic Cylinder LON-104

Total: 40 Cards

Killer Deck

heavenly light

By - Augustine Choyy, a.k.a. Wartortle32

My mission was to create an original deck and have it be competitive too. My method was create a variant of the Beatdown style, which is currently one of the most successful deck types. The result is one of my more successful creations, a light themed Beatdown deck with a little flavor of hand disruption.

It is both original and competitive. I also needed to add a theme of hand disruption because drawing all support cards for light monsters makes this deck rather slow. If you're going to be slow, you might as well slow down your opponent to even the playing field.

First of all, it shouldn't be too difficult to get all of the card for this deck. It doesn't use most of the ultra and secret rare like most Beatdowns (Gemini Elf, Goblin Attack Force). Most of the monsters I'm using are commons or rares.

Monsters

As you can see, I've chosen Hysteric Fairy and Thunder Nyan Nyan as my main forces for beatdown. These two are the strongest lower level monsters, so it wasn't too hard to select them.

Hysteric Fairy's attack is decent and its Effect can be nice if you use something like Change of Heart or sacrifice a Sangan/WOTBF. Thunder Nyan Nyan has one of the strongest attacks for a level 4 monster. The Effect of this monster, while detrimental in other decks, works perfect here. Almost all the monsters I have are Light These will almost never be played face up, so it doesn't hurt Thunder Nyan Nyan.

In fact, its Effect actually makes this deck stronger. If your opponent wants to take control of one of your monsters, it would be almost impossible for him or her to take this monster since Light monsters aren't seen much anywhere.

If your opponent wants to take control of Thunder Nyan Nyan, he will need a clear field or this monster will be destroyed. In any case, the result is you will lose less LP.

The key to this deck is that you must get out Luminous Spark as soon as you can. You will be very vulnerable without it, since Light monsters can't compare in sheer strength with regular Beatdown monsters. With Luminous Spark in play, your Nyan Nyans are a 2400, strong enough to take out Jinzo.

Your Hysteric Fairies are at 2300, strong enough to take out GAFs. Plus, the Shining Angels are there

AIRKNIGHT PARSHATH

[FAIRY / EFFECT]
When this card attacks with an ATK higher than the DEF of your opponent's Defense Position monster, inflict the difference as Battle Damage to your opponent's Life Points. When this card inflicts Battle Damage to your opponent's Life Points, draw 1 card from your Deck.

ATK/1900 DEF/1400

LOD-062

©1996 KAZUKI TAKAHASHI

18036057

Monsters (17)
3x Thunder Nyan Nyan (LOD – 059)
3x Hysteric Fairy (LON – 042)
2x White Magical Hat (MRD – 016)
2x Shining Angel (MRL – 088)
1x Airknight Parshath (LOD – 062)
1x Soul of Purity and Light (LON – 066)
1x Magician of Faith (MRD – 036)
1x Cyber Jar (MRL – 077)
1x Fiber Jar (LOD – 056)
1x Witch of the Black Forest (MRD – 016)
1x Sangan (MRD – 069)

Magics (18)
1x Pot of Greed (LOB – 119)
1x Monster Reborn (LOB – 118)
1x Change of Heart (MRD – 060)
1x Snatch Steal (MRL – 036)
1x Heavy Storm (MRD – 142)
1x Harpies Feather Duster (SDD -003)
2x MST (MRL – 047)
1x Dark Hole (LOB – 052)
1x Raigeki (LOB – 053)
3x Luminous Spark (MRL – 100)
1x Nobleman of Crossout (PSV – 034)
1x The Forceful Sentry (MRL – 045)
1x Delinquent Duo (MRL – 039)
1x Graceful Charity (SDP – 040)
1x Premature Burial (PSV – 037)

Traps (8)
1x Torrential Tribute (LON – 025)
1x Imperial Order (PSV – 104)
1x Call of the Haunted (PSV – 012)
1x Magic Jammer (MRD – 128)
1x 7 tools of the Bandit (MRD – 129)
1x Robbin Goblin (MRD – 135)
1x Mirror Force (MRD – 138)
1x Magic Cylinder (LON – 104)

Total: 43 cards

to provide more defense. When they get killed, it can pull out another monster to defend your LP.

Soul of Purity and Light works great in this deck as it is a Special Summon monster and is absolutely deadly when Luminous Spark is in play. Fiber __ is there to give you a way out of a sticky situation. It can provide __u with a clean slate and a better hand.

Finally, the White Magical Hats are used to add to the Hand __sruption theme. As a side note, I did not include Yata Garasu in this __eck even though it is a hand disruption deck. I tried using it deck __d found that it clashes with the Light theme. You can add one and __e if it works for you.

__agics

Most of the Magic cards are fairly self explanatory. I have the necessary staples, plus the required cards for a hand dis-__ption decks. Another key to this deck is to attack quickly and empty all of the useful cards out of your opponent's hand __ he or she can't do anything against you.

An early attack by White Magical Hat, combined with Delinquent Duo or The Forceful Sentry, is the ideal situation. To __ll this off, you need to clear the opponent's M/T zone.

__ decided to go with the combo of one Duster, one Heavy Storm and two MST. You'll find that this should be adequate __ last you the game. Also included are the necessary monster removal Magic cards. I did not include any equip Magic __owerup cards because I didn't want to expand the deck.

Besides, if you can get out Luminous Spark, your main attack monsters should have no problem wiping the field clear of __pponent monsters.

__raps

There are no surprises here. You'll find all the staple Trap cards. I included a Magic Jammer to help protect the __minous Sparks, as you'll be a sitting duck without it. I also have a 7 Tools because this deck isn't using Jinzo and you __ed some sort of trap protection.

The last note of interest is the Robbin Goblin, which fits the hand disruption theme well. A rush of monsters combined __th this card can completely empty out your opponent's hand. ■

Killer Deck

exodia

By Ken Jackson

The Exodia deck has been around since the beginning and each new expansion seems to bring its own twist to the archetype. Sets like Pharaoh's Servant and Metal Raiders added a lot of key cards to Exodia while others, like Labyrinth of Nightmare and the new Legacy of Darkness, brought in cards that give Exodia a hard time.

There are several variants of Exodia as well, the most common being defensive. This includes a lot of Magic and Trap cards designed to prevent your opponent from attacking. Also, some monsters that have 3000 DEF are used as walls.

The offensive Exodia adds in elements of a Beatdown to hold its own, while drawing the pieces. Then there's my favorite, card The Recursion Exodia. This one is different from the others as it uses a kamikaze technique to destroy the search cards faster, and then various monster recursion cards to bring them back.

First let's look at a solid Exodia deck, and then let's take a look at some cards from Legacy of Darkness that any Exodia player does not like to see, and ways to counter them.

Ok, so let's analyze this deck, shall we? The premise is simple. If you get one Spear Cretin in your Grave and one in play, then you have an infinite wall if you are attacked. It's very good with Card of Safe Return, as each time you are attacked you draw a card.

Use all your monster recursion (Reborn, Call of the Haunted, Shallow Grave, Premature Burial) to bring back your Sangan, Witch, (Don't forget to draw cards…) Or, if the situation warrants, Spear Cretin, Magician of Faith, or Penguin Soldier.

Also, one of the most effective strategies in Exodia, albeit one of the least used, is Kamikaze. Don't be averse to running your Witch or Sangan into a Gemini Elf or Bazoo or

something. 900 life points is a small price to pay for a precious limb. I mean after all, that's the entire goal o the deck, right?

Now that we've seen the deck, lets see what cards from Legacy of Darkness can help or hurt it.

First, we see a void of cards that wi help this Exodia deck. In fact, the on card that might even be a REMOTE help is Fiber Jar. If you have room, yo can always put one of these in your hand and only use it in life or death situations (like you have 1000 life points left, and you only have one limb.) I think in that case it's safe to panic and restart the game.

In most situations, you'll want to avoid playing Fiber Jar like the plague. Nothing is more frustrating than when you have 4 pieces in your hand and you're about to go for the last one, and your opponent flips over that Fiber Jar. Of course when this happens, you DO have your Solemn Judgment or Royal Command set, don't you?

Other cards that hurt Exodia are those that remove cards from play. If you thought that Kycoo was bad, Fiend Comedian makes it look like child's play. On a correct coin flip, your opponent gets to remove your entire Graveyard from play… doubled with Second Coin Toss, there's a 75% chance of it happening. There goes your infinite Spear Cretin wall, or the Limbs you stored there, with your Painfu Choice.

Dark Ruler of Ha Des is not to be overlooked. When it's out and about, all monsters destroyed by Ha Des, or any other Fiend type, don't get to use their Effects. You can fo get about getting your Sangan or Witch's Effects. No more Spear Cretin of Nimble Momonga either… all of which are crucial to the overall smoothness of the deck.

Drawing is also essential, so if your opponent starts using Yata-Garasu, or Drop Off, you could be in for a rough time Drop Off is a Trap that makes you discard the card you draw at the beginning of your turn, no questions asked. And of course Yata just prevents you from drawing at all.

Drop Off is more easily dealt with, as its only a one time

not, where as Yata can keep coming back to haunt you. Again, if you're in trouble, don't think twice about using that Solemn Judgment and paying half your life in order to destroy the bird. It'll be worth it if you can draw your last piece.

Exiled Force is also a strong force to be reckoned with in any deck, but much more so against Exodia. Exiled Force allows your opponent to sacrifice Exiled Force in order to destroy one of your monsters. Face up. Face down. Attack. Defense. It's all the same to Exiled Force.

It can stymie your Spear Cretin wall or Penguin Soldier, bouncing faster than you can say 'I wish I had a Trap Hole…' Again, in the deck the way it is, the most effective way to counter this is Solemn Judgment. However if you find yourself running up against Exile Force a lot, and I'm sure you will, you might want to add in some Trap Holes, or even a Prohibition, as a safety from your dreaded cards.

The last dangerous card for Exodia Players is Bubble Crash. This Trap card can only be activated when you have six or more cards in play and in your hand combined. Your opponent plays Bubble Crash and you have to discard your precious cards until you only have five total in play and in your hand. Not the best way to clear up your field, is it? When going against this play, your best bet is to chain. Chain whatever you can. It clears your field and counts towards Bubble Crash's five-card limit. Chain those MSTs to get rid of some of your opponent's cards. Chain Call of the Haunted, get back your Witch/Sangan, and then destroy it. Hey, why not get a piece of Exodia out of it?'

Overall, Legacy of Darkness makes life more difficult for Exodia, but it's nothing a seasoned Exodia veteran can't handle. Make sure to know your deck, know as much about your opponent's deck as possible, and know the popular cards in your area. Remember the cards that can hurt you, plus the ones that are popular in your area, and tweak your deck to counter them. ∎

Exodia Recursion:
42 Cards

Monsters: 17
1x Exodia the Forbidden One (LOB-124/DDS-003)
1x Left Arm of the Forbidden One (LOB-123)
1x Right Arm of the Forbidden One (LOB-122)
1x Left Leg of the Forbidden One (LOB-121)
1x Right Leg of the Forbidden One (LOB-120)
1x Witch of the Black Forest (MRD-116/SDP-014)
1x Sangan (MRD-069/SDJ-019)
2x Magician of Faith (MRD-036/SDJ-017)
3x Spear Cretin (MRL-087)
3x Nimble Momonga (MRL-086)
1x Penguin Soldier (SDJ-022)
1x Sinister Serpent (SDD-002)

Magic: 11
1x Monster Reborn (LOB-118/SDJ-035/SDK-036/SDP-035/SDY-030)
2x Shallow Grave (PSV-036)
1x Premature Burial (PSV-037)
2x Graceful Charity (SDP-040)
1x Pot of Greed (LOB-119/TP3-014)
1x Card of Safe Return (LON-029)
1x Mystical Space Typhoon (MRL-047/SPD-032)
1x Painful Choice (MRL-049)
1x Dark Hole (LOB-052/SDJ-026/SDK-022/SDP-026/SDY-022)

Trap: 14
2x Backup Soldier (PSV-028)
2x Gravity Bind (PSV-073)
1x Imperial Order (PSV-104)
1x Call of the Haunted (PSV-012)
1x Mirror Force (MRD-138)
2x Magic Jammer (MRD-128/SDP-048)
2x Solemn Judgment (MRD-127)
3x Jar of Greed (LON-047)

Killer Deck

SILENCE FIEND!!!

By Adam Forristal

With the release of Legacy of Darkness, many new sub-type specific cards are available. Many of these cards are beneficial to Fiend monsters. As such, the Fiend deck needs an overhaul, incorporating at least three or four of these new cards.

Fiend decks can be very devastating when put together correctly. Most of the cards are fairly straightforward, so I'll only put in explanations for the controversial cards, or the ones that need explaining. The deck I've compiled is as follows:

The Bistro Butcher, La Jinn, and Opticlops – these are all Level Four, Fiend, 1800 attackers. So, Effects or not, they're all in the deck.

Kuriboh - Kuriboh's Effect serves two purposes. First and foremost, it can save you in dire situations. Secondly, Kuriboh happens to be a Fiend. Kuriboh's Effect means that it goes from your hand to your graveyard. Why is this useful? Dark Necrofear, the heart and soul of this deck, can only be special summoned by removing three Fiends in your graveyard from play. Kuriboh fits this role nicely, as you can use the Effect to send it away, and then use Kuriboh again to bring out Dark Necrofear

Cyber Jar – This card is here for speed. It nets you five new cards, speeding up this fairly slow deck.

Winged Minion – This is another controversial card, but I'm including it anyway. Winged Minion is another Legacy of Darkness card. Its Effect enables you to boost the ATK and DEF of a Fiend monster by 700 points. When this is done, you will be in good shape as this is a huge, permanent bonus.

ark Ruler Ha Des – Another beauti-
l Legacy of Darkness card. Level Six,
50/1500, and a great Effect. I have
e of these, but you can interchange
s with Summoned Skull. As long as
u have a combined total of three
etween Dark Ruler Ha Des and
mmoned Skull), than everything's
od.

top of the fairly high attack and
eat Effect, this card has another
vantage in this deck. Almost all the
onsters are Fiend type, so tributing a
onster to bring this one out will put
other Fiend in the graveyard for
mmoning Dark Necrofear.

ark Necrofear – The heart of the
ck and the purpose of having the 38
her cards. Dark Necrofear may not
ve the strongest attack (2200), but
defense is good (2800) and its Effect
amazing.

vords of Revealing Light – Like I
d earlier, this deck is going to be
ow. SORL is here to stall your oppo-
nt so you can get the cards you
ed.

arpie's Feather Duster – The
igeki of Magic and Traps, this card
as one of the three released in Yu-Gi-
h! Worldwide Edition: Stairway to the
estined Duel for the Gameboy
vance. It might be hard to get your
nds on, but it's a great card.

rd Destruction – I keep talking
out how slow this deck is going to
. This card, again, is here to speed it
.

Painful Choice – Simple, just select at
least four Fiends, and three are guaranteed to go to the graveyard, making
it much easier to summon Dark
Necrofear. Also, this'll remove five
cards from your deck, speeding it up in
the process.

Bark of Dark Ruler – A great trap for
all Fiend monsters. At the low cost of
600 LP, Summoned Skull can beat a
Blue Eyes White Dragon. While I don't
recommend relying on this card, it can
be a big help.

Call of the Haunted - It's Monster
Reborn in Trap form. I recommend
combining it with Giant Trunade
(Sidedeck Alert) to remove the negative
After Effect (and you get to use it a sec-
ond time).

Imperial Order – This'll save you in a
few situations. Don't like the continuous cost? Use it once and don't pay.
It's like another Magic Jammer

Magic Jammer – A One-Time-Use
Imperial Order, this card may win
games for you (by canceling out a card
your opponent needs to win).

Magic Cylinder – It can negate one
attack AND do Life Point damage? I
think so! This card may win games, or
at least put you in a great situation.
Such is the reason this is restricted to
one. ■

Monsters
3x The Bistro Butcher MRD-
108
3x La Jinn The Mystical Genie
SDK-026
3x Opticlops LOD-009
3x Kuriboh MRD-071
1x Cyber Jar MRL-077
2x Winged Minion LOD-005
1x Dark Ruler Ha Des LOD-001
2x Summoned Skull MRD-
003/SDY
2x Dark Necrofear LON-065

Magic
1x Swords of Revealing Light
LOB-101
1x Dark Hole LOB-052/All
Starter Decks
1x Raigeki LOB-053
1x Heavy Storm MRD-142
1x Harpie's Feather Duster
SDD-003 (promo card)
1x Card Destruction SDY-042
1x Graceful Charity SDP-040
1x United We Stand LON-049
1x Painful Choice MRL-049
1x Change of Heart MRD-
060/SDY, SDK, SDP
1x Pot of Greed LOB-119/TP3-
014
1x Monster Reborn LOB-
118/All Starter Decks

Trap
2x Bark of Dark Ruler LOD-010
1x Mirror Force MRD-138
1x Call of the Haunted PSV-
012
1x Imperial Order PSV-104
2x Magic Jammer MRD-
128/SDP
1x Magic Cylinder LON-104

Killer Deck

THE FIRE PRINCESS

By Ken Jackson

The Fire Princess has always been a rogue deck. It's not consistent enough to be a mainstream archetype, but it's also too powerful to ignore. For those of you who are unaware, the Fire Princess premise is simple. However, it relies on a number of factors to be effective.

The goal is to get out one or more Fire Princesses and several other cards to gain your Life Points. With the Fire Princess on the field, each time you gain life, your opponent loses life. If you have three Fire Princesses in play, that's 1500 direct damage EVERY TIME YOU GAIN LIFE. For example, let's say you have one Solemn Wish in play and a Fire Princess. It would mean a 500 increase in Life Points for you, and 500 damage to your opponent. If you have two Solemn Wishes and two Fire Princesses… you're gaining 1000 life points, and your opponent is losing 2000! (1000 from each Fire Princess since you gained life twice.)

As you can see, it can become quite powerful and very quick… once it gets started. I want to thank Julia and Jeff for letting me analyze their Fire Princess decks and tweak them a bit:

As you can see, there are slightly more cards in this deck than a standard deck, but again, that's how a Fire Princess deck runs. Let's take a quick look at the deck and the reasoning for the cards.

There are a number of life-gaining monsters in the deck. Cure Mermaid and Dancing Fairy both gain life during your Standby phase if they are face up on the field. Cure Mermaid's Effect takes place when it's in Attack or Defense, while Dancing Fairy has to be in Defense.

This is where the Trap card Light of Intervention comes into play. As long as Light of Intervention is out, monsters can't be set face down. They all have to be played face up in either Attack or Defense mode. This makes it a lot easier to bring out your life gaining monsters (or even Fire Princess for that matter), but still have them safe from attack.

Marie the Fallen One does the same trick, but whenever she's in the Graveyard at the start of your turn, you gain 200 life. The trick with Marie is NOT to put her into play if you can help it. She's a Tribute monster, so that forces you to get rid of one of your other monsters. You want to have all of them in play as long as possible.

You need to use Marie with your Tribute to the Doomed or Graceful Charity. The easiest way to get her in

FIRE PRINCESS

[PYRO / EFFECT]
Inflict 500 points of Direct Damage to your opponent's Life Points each time you increase your own Life Points.

ATK/1300 DEF/1500

©1996 KAZUKI TAKAHASHI

LON-034

...he Graveyard is to use her as payment for another card... and get something out of it!

The Cannon Soldiers are there for cleanup. Near the end of the game just drop a Cannon Soldier and sacrifice all your monsters for a quick 2500 damage to finish the game. The Scapegoats can aid in this last strike. They also can protect you from direct attacks earlier in the game, if you can't draw the monsters you need.

Overall, once you get this setup, it's a very quick and painful deck. Ideally, if you have three Fire Princess in play, along with two other life gaining monsters, plus your three Marie in the Grave and three Solemn Wishes down... you caused 12,000 damage in one turn! Of course, the chance of this circumstance is slim, but it's something you should aim to complete!

Now we need to discuss the downside. There is one Trap in Legacy of Darkness that renders Fire Princess not only useless, but turns it against you. I'm talking about Bad Reaction to Simochi. Sadly, I've used up all my Simochi jokes in previous writings, so let's cut to the chase. Simochi is bad news.

As long as Simochi is out, instead of gaining life, you lose it. Every single Cure Mermaid and Marie the Fallen One is now working in unison against you. No longer do you get to reap the benefits of gaining thousands of life points per turn, instead you have to feel the burn you were putting on your opponent.

The simplest way to deal with Simochi

is with Mystical Space Typhoon. Players seem to have fun flipping Simochi over on your Standby phase, just before the life gain kicks in. Your reaction to this? MST it. Play it from your hand. Play it from your field. Just. Play it. The sooner you can get rid of Simochi, the better. It must be gone in one or two turns, or it will spell trouble.

Another deadly card in LOD, although not as bad, is the increasingly popular Spear Dragon. It has 1900 ATK and a built in Fairy Meteor Crush. What that means is even if your monsters are in Defense, they'll still be taking hits. You must always have an ace up your sleeve, or at least a Tribute to the Doomed.

You can take care of these nuisances by using TttD, Mirror Force, or just block them outright with Messenger of Peace or Gravity Bind. They can't hurt you if they can't attack you.

The last card to watch out for is the same card that can both help or hurt any deck. It's Fiber Jar. Nothing hurts worse than taking seven turns to set up the perfect field, you have your Princesses, Mermaids, and Fairies galore, and then... your opponent flips Fiber Jar. It's not a pretty site.

Of course, Fiber jar can be countered if you have Light of Intervention or Ceasefire. With Ceasefire, it not only counters but does damage. On the other hand, a Fiber Jar is a nice way to get a fresh start. It is especially helpful when you have 15,000 Life Points and your opponent has 6,000...

If you want to try a deck that isn't the standard Beatdown or Exodia, give Fire Princess a shot. It can hold it's own in most cases, it is highly customizable, and the essential cards are relatively easy to come by. If you don't want to

go with the monster heavy route, try a bunch of life gaining Magic cards, like Dian Keto or Red Medicine.

I saw someone with a Fire Princess variant that used Simochi plus a number of cards that forced his opponent to gain life, like Rain of Mercy, Upstart Goblin, and Eye of Truth. This is one of the most versatile deck types out there, and you can have a lot of fun with it, as well as annoy a lot of people!
-k ∎

Fire Princess: 50 Cards
Monsters: 22
3x Fire Princess (LON-034)
3x Marie the Fallen One (LON-046)
3x Cure Mermaid (LON-041)
3x Dancing Fairy (LON-038)
3x Spear Cretin (MRL-087)
3x Nimble Momonga (MRL-086)
2x Cannon Soldier (MRD-106)
1x Fiber Jar (LOD-056)
1x Witch of the Black Forest (MRD-116/SDP-014)

Magic: 15
2x Mystical Space Typhoon (MRL-047/SPD-032)
2x Messenger of Peace (MRL-102)
2x Scapegoat (SDJ-041)
2x Graceful Charity (SDP-040)
2x Tribute to the Doomed (MRD-057)
1x Premature Burial (PSV-037)
1x Raigeki (LOB-053)
1x Pot of Greed (LOB-119/TP3-014)
1x Swords of Revealing Light (LOB-101)
1x Monster Reborn (LOB-118/SDJ-035/SDK-036/SDP-035/SDY-030)

Trap: 13
2x Light of Intervention (PSV-031)
3x Solemn Wishes (PSV-055)
2x Gravity Bind (PSV-073)
2x Magic Jammer (MRD-128/SDP-048)
1x Imperial Order (PSV-104)
1x Mirror Force (MRD-138)
2x Ceasefire (PSV-030)

Killer Deck

THE BIRD DECK

By Chris Schroeder

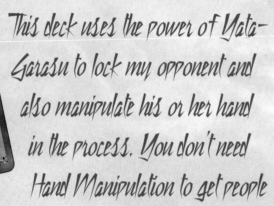

This deck uses the power of Yata-Garasu to lock my opponent and also manipulate his or her hand in the process. You don't need Hand Manipulation to get people into the bird lock, but it makes it easier to lock your opponent in it. It uses an old card back from the Yugi Starter deck, Last Will. Plus, Share The Pain from Metal Raiders. They combo well with Last Will.

Also, I follow the Japanese Restrictions on new sets until Upper Deck releases a new restriction list. Yata-Garasu and Fairy Injection Lily are limited to one per deck. It's why you won't see three Yata-Garasus in this deck.

This deck contains all the cards you see in any deck such as Monster Reborn, Raigeki, Imperial Order, Cyber Jar, etc. It includes Yata-Garasu, which is part of the deck because it can easily lock your opponent and win you the game.

It also has White Magical Hat, Hayabusa Knight and Fairy Injection Lily. If the bird happens to be destroyed, these monsters are your back up plan to win the duel. Instead of trying to lock them, you can use these creatures to take out your opponent's remaining Life Points.

Since the Injection Lily is a 3400 attack power creature, when you pay 2000 she can take out the basic level four monster with 1800-1900 or even a Jinzo. With the White Magical Hats and Hayabusa Knights, you can combo these with Robbin' Goblin to knock out two cards from your opponent's hand and do damage to his or her Life Points. Losing two cards from the hand can be very effective, since your opponent might have a monster removal card or another level four creature waiting to knock out your Hat or Knight.

Twin Headed Behemoth is two monsters in one. When it is destroyed, it comes back as a special summon with 1000/1000 ATK/DEF creature at the end of the turn when it was destroyed. Though it's only once per game, it's an effective attacker for 1500 ATK. Also, Exile Force clears a monster off the field with its Effect, while the Witch and Sangan search for creatures. Of course no deck should be left without Cyber Jar.

As you can see, Magic cards are a big part

Hat and I get to hit my opponent and knock cards out of his or her hand. Since most opponents only play one Trap Hole or Torrential Tribute at a time, he or she can be caught off guard with this.

Share the Pain helps Last Will work more effectively. You must tribute one of your monsters and your opponent tributes a monster as well. It's nice monster removal, since it can take out face down monsters, and there aren't usually more than two monsters on the field in this game anyway. It helps you trigger Last Will's Effect to special summon a monster onto to the field, plus you still may have a regular summon as well.

Mystical Space Typhoon, Heavy Storm and Harpie's Feather Duster are here because they help clear the field of those pesky Trap cards. It may seem like overload, but there are a lot of Magic/Trap cards that stay out on the field. It's necessary to have a lot of Trap and Magic removal.

Last but not least are the trap cards. Robbin' Goblin is a key Trap card in this deck. It helps your monsters knock out cards from your opponent's hand every time they do Life Points of damage during battle. Torrential Tribute is the best Trap card when it comes to monsters. Any kind of summon lets you activate this card to clear the field of monsters (face up or face down).

Drop Off is a new card from Legacy of Darkness that has a tough Effect. Your opponent must immediately discard the card he or she has drawn at the beginning of the turn. It can lock up your opponent for one turn if played correctly. Your monsters first discard cards from your opponent's hand, and then Drop Off knocks another card out of his or her hand. Just when he or she really needs to recover from the last attacks, it's the perfect opportu-

of this deck. It has all the staple Magic cards like Raigeki, Monster Reborn, Swords of Revealing light, etc. It also has the key Magic cards that can take out cards from the hand like Delinquent Duo and Confiscation.

Card Destruction eliminates your hand and draws the same amount, which is effective in the beginning of the first turn of the game. Your opponent can't stop it since he or she hasn't had a turn to set any Trap cards.

Graceful Charity and Pot of Greed are there to help you draw out the right cards. Last Will is an old card that I also have found to be helpful in special summoning the monsters I need. Most of them are less than 1500 ATK points making them perfect for this type of deck. Whenever you lose a monster because of Torrential Tribute or Trap Hole, you can use this card to special summon a monster onto the field.

Let's say my opponent Trap Hole's my Hayabusa Knight, and I was planning on a Robbin' Goblin combo. Last Will lets me bring out either another Hayabusa Knight or a White Magical

Monsters: 13
Yata-Garasu - LOD-000
Fairy Injection Lily - LOD-100
Exiled Force - LOD - LOD-023
Cyber Jar - MRL-077
Witch Of The Black Forest - MRD-116
Sangan - MRD-069
Twin-Headed Behemoth - LOD-063
White Magical Hat x3 - MRD-016
Hayabusa Knight x3 - PSV-086
Magic: 21
Heavy Storm - MRD-142
Harpie's Feather Duster - SDD-003
Pot of Greed - LOB-119
Swords of Revealing Light - LOB-101
Change of Heart - MRD-060
Card Destruction - SDY-042
Graceful Charity - SDP-040
Monster Reborn - LOB-118
Dark Hole - LOB-052
Raigeki - LOB-053
Confiscation - MRL-038
Delinquent Duo - MRL-039
The Forceful Sentry - MRL-045
Last Will x3 - SDY-039
Share The Pain x2 - MRD-140
Mystical Space Typhoon x3 - MRL-047

Trap: 8
Torrential Tribute x2 - LON-025
Mirror Force - MRD-138
Imperial Order - PSV-104
Robbin' Goblin x2 - MRD-135
Drop Off x2 - LOD-097

nity to use Yata-Garasu and lock your opponent.

Drop Off is difficult to stop. The only way you can prevent it is by using Seven Tools, Solemn Judgment or a well-played MST (Mystical Space Typhoon). Imperial Order and Mirror Force are staple Trap cards and should never be left out of a deck.

So there you have it. The newest type of deck to hit the tournament scene for Yu-Gi-Oh! There are a lot of other variant decks besides this one. There are some decks that use Yata-Garasu, just hoping to get lucky and lock out their opponent. Believe me, it's an easy thing to do. ∎

Killer Deck

BURN!!!

By Evan Vargas, a.k.a. SandTrap

Here's a Burn/Direct Damage deck for you to consider. The focus is to deplete the opponent's Life Points as fast as possible.

Spear Dragon and Cannon Soldier are two very effective ways to quickly deplete the opponent's LPs (Life Points), and thus win the game. In the tournament scene, many duelists use Goblin Attack Forces (GAFs) and Spear Dragons, as the metagame is filled with Beatdown decks. Spear Dragon is a great choice to play in this kind of deck. Against other GAFs and Spear Dragons, each hit can do 1900 LP damage because GAF/Spear go into defense mode after they attack.

Let your opponent attack, then summon a Spear Dragon and nail him or her for 1900. Also, Spear Dragon is very effective against the face down monsters that are often played, such as Magician of Faith, Morphing Jar, Cyber Jar, Fiber Jar, Sinister Serpent, Nimble Momonga, etc.

Cannon Soldier is the other monster necessary in a Direct Damage/Burn deck. With Cannon Soldier and Scapegoat in combination, you can inflict 2000 LP damage to your opponent for each Scapegoat used. Place Scapegoat face down on your previous turn, and let your opponent take his or her turn. Before they finish, flip over your Scapegoat and activate it. Since it is now your turn, you can freely summon a Cannon Soldier and launch all the tokens for 2000 LPs. Another use for Cannon Soldier is to use Change of Heart or Snatch Steal on an opponent's monster, summon your own Cannon Soldier, and attack with both of them for a nice amount of damage. Plus, you can launch your opponent's monster before the end of your turn. Your opponent won't gain control of his or her monster on the next turn (Change of Heart), nor will he or she gain 1000 LPs from Snatch Steal.

Fiber Jar can also be of great benefit in this deck. Let's say you are winning the duel by 4000 LPs, you're almost out of cards in your hand and field, and your opponent is about to make a comeback. Get Fiber to the field and get it flipped. Now you have a fresh start and a big lead in the game! If you can keep repeating this process of doing

SPEAR DRAGON

MAGIC CYLINDER

Monsters –14–
[3] Spear Dragon (LOD-035)
[3] Cannon Soldier (MRD-106)
[2] Mystic Tomato (MRL-094)
[1] Jinzo (PSV-000)
[1] Witch of the Black Forest (MRD-116)
[1] Sangan (MRD-069)
[1] Sinister Serpent (SDD-002)
[1] Yata-Garasu (LOD-000)
[1] Fiber Jar (LOD-056)

Magic –21–
[1] Raigeki (LOB-053)
[1] Dark Hole (LOB-052)
[1] Pot of Greed (LOB-119)
[1] Change of Heart (MRD-060)
[1] Monster Reborn (LOB-118)
[1] Harpie's Feather Duster (SDD-003)
[1] Heavy Storm (MRD-142)
[3] Mystical Space Typhoon (MRL-047)
[2] Graceful Charity (SDP-040)
[3] Scapegoat (SDJ-041)
[1] Creature Swap (LOD-081)
[1] Snatch Steal (MRL-036)
[1] Premature Burial (PSV-037)
[1] Forceful Sentry (MRL-045)
[1] Confiscation (MRD-038)
[1] Delinquent Duo (MRL-039)

Traps –5–
[1] Mirror Force (MRD-138)
[1] Magic Cylinder (LON-104)
[1] Waboku (SDY-040)
[1] Call of the Haunted (PSV-012)
[1] Imperial Order (PSV-104)

–40– Cards Total

irect damage and flipping Fiber Jar, it may be difficult for your opponent to win.

Mystic Tomato is a great card to have in this deck as well. When it is destroyed in battle, it can search for Cannon Soldier, Witch of the Black Forest, or Sangan. By getting out Cannon Soldier, you can set up the above-mentioned Scapegoat launch. Or, you can bring out Witch or Sangan so that you can search through your deck much faster and find the cards that you need.

Also, 1400 ATK isn't half bad, as it can take out a lot of monsters being played, such as Flip Effect monsters, Sinister Serpent, Sangan, Witch, Marauding Captain, DEF mode GAFs/Spear Dragons, etc. You need to watch out for those 1800+ monsters, but recall that you may want the tomatoes to die in battle so you can search your deck. Either way, it's a win-win situation.

The other monsters are there for obvious reasons. Witch and Sangan search through the deck. Jinzo is the trap negator, and pretty strong as well. Sinister Serpent is great with Graceful Charity, White Magical Hat is for hand disruption and Delinquent Duo is a great monster to stall with, etc. Yata-Garasu, with help from a little hand disruption, can lock your opponent and win the game.

Magic Cards

Many of the restricted cards play important roles in the deck, or any

deck for that matter. The staples: Raigeki, Dark Hole, Pot of Greed, Change of Heart, Monster Reborn, and Harpie's Feather Duster are all there. Three Mystical Space Typhoons (MSTs) and Heavy Storm keep your opponent with as little support as possible. The MSTs can also chain to an opponent's Imperial Order, making it more useful.

Snatch Steal helps with Cannon Soldier, as does Premature Burial. The hand disruption acts as pre-negation, taking cards away before they can be used. They also allow the player to see what the opponent's options are, and thus allow the player to predict what the opponent will do.

The three Scapegoats help Cannon Soldier do damage, plus they can act as a wall against deadly attacks. They let you stall while you prepare for the upcoming turns and attacks. Creature Swap works unbelievably well with Scapegoat. With a few tokens on the field, switch one of them into attack mode, and play Creature Swap. You will have gained one of your opponent's monsters, as well as doing some nice damage by attacking the super weak Sheep Token with the monster you took.

Of course we also have two Graceful Charities. The faster a deck, the better.

Trap Cards

The Trap cards are few in number but great in value. Mirror Force is Raigeki in Trap form. Magic Cylinder allows for some nice LP damage as well as protection for one of your monsters. Call of the Haunted can be used

as tribute bait for Cannon Soldier, or to bring back a powerful monster like Spear Dragon or Jinzo. Imperial Order is the best anti-Magic card ever.

Waboku helps protect your DEF mode Spear Dragons so they last another turn, plus to hopefully do more damage. Waboku can also be used to protect your LPs, slow or stop a Yata lock, or act as m/t removal bait.

I hope I have explained how this deck works. In the right hands, it can be quite formidable. And with many decks using cards like Delinquent Duo, Confiscation, and Injection Fairy Lily, depleting the opponent's LPs shouldn't be too difficult a job. Get to it. ■

Cheap @$$ Deck
CLOWN CONTROL

By Vijay Seixas, a.k.a. SomeGuy

I know that there are a lot of Yu-Gi-Oh! players who simply don't have the funds to build a deck that contains 30-35 foil cards. Here is your chance to build a casual version of Clown Control that consists of mostly Commons! This version only has seven Rare cards to be exact, and no foils. Without further adieu, I bring you: Cheap @$$ Clown Control –

Keep in mind that this version is nowhere near as strong as the version presented earlier in this book, but the general strategy is the same. Keep your opponent at bay with Gravity Bind and control them with Dream Clown, Crass Clown, and White Magical Hat. This budgeted version of the deck runs tons of Monster Removal in the form of Dark Hole, Offerings to the Doomed, Fissure, Skull Lair, 4-Starred Ladybug of Doom, Dream Clown, and Crass Clown. You should always have a clear path for your level three weenies to finish off your opponent.

Monster Cards

The monster section is basic. We have our monster control cards, Dream Clown, Crass Clown, and 4-Starred Ladybug of Doom; and, we have our Hand control card, White Magical Hat. Hayabusa Knight is used as offense and deals some nice Life Point damage.

Witch of the Black Forest and Sangan are the setup cards. Magician of Faith is your basic Magic support. Reusing your restricted Magic cards is always nice. Cyber Jar is present for when you're in a tight situation. Just hope your opponent doesn't get a huge advantage from it.

Magic Cards

Pot of Greed, Monster Reborn, Change of Heart, and Dark Hole are self-explanatory. They are extremely

DREAM CLOWN

EARTH

[WARRIOR / EFFECT]
When this card is changed from Attack Position to Defense Position, select and destroy 1 monster on your opponent's side of the field.

ATK/1200 DEF/ 900
©1996 KAZUKI TAKAHASHI
MRD-080
13215230

good in their own way. Offerings to the Doomed and Fissure are both decent Monster Removal cards. Offerings to the Doomed is a great way to deal with an opposing Jinzo as well.

The Warrior Returning Alive allows you to use a destroyed Dream Clown of Hayabusa Knight over and over again. Heart of Clear Water is your main Dream Clown support. Although it can be used on other monsters as well as Crass Clown. It also works very well when you can't seem to draw Gravity Bind.

Mystical Space Typhoon is much too good not to use. Luckily they made Mystical Space Typhoon a Common, or else low budget decks wouldn't have any good Magic and Trap removal.

Trap Cards

Gravity Bind is a large part of the deck, that's why I've included three. Drawing one early in the game helps immensely. Moreover, there's always Heart of Clear Water if you have a Dream Clown but haven't drawn a Gravity Bind.

Skull Lair is excellent mass-removal. It can work like, or even better than, a Raigeki. Just be aware of Fiber Jar. Your opponent can gain a major advantage if they flip Fiber Jar after you've been mass using Skull Lair.

Lastly, we have Magic Jammer. Your opponent will attempt to destroy your Gravity Bind throughout the game, so it's best to save your Magic Jammer for when they do. Although you shouldn't be afraid to Magic Jammer other powerful cards if the situation calls for it.

Money wise, this is an exceptional deck. Just don't expect to beat the top players in your area. Although you'll have a great time giving it a try. The best thing to remember? Good decks in the Yu-Gi-Oh! Collectable Card Game don't have to cost you hundreds of dollars to be solid competitors and a lot of fun. ∎

-Monster Cards- 17
3x Dream Clown MRD-080 & SDP-017 Common
3x White Magical Hat SDJ-021 Common
2x Crass Clown MRD-078 Common
2x Hayabusa Knight PSV-086 Rare
2x 4-Starred Ladybug of Doom PSV-088 Common
2x Magician of Faith SDJ-017 Common
1x Witch of the Black Forest SDP-014 Common
1x Sangan SDJ-019 Common
1x Cyber Jar MRL-077 Common

-Magic Cards- 16
1x Pot of Greed TP3-014 Common
1x Monster Reborn SDJ-035, SDK-036, SDP-035, & SDY-030 Common
1x Change of Heart SDJ-030, SDP-030, & SDY-032 Common
1x Dark Hole SDJ-026, SDK-022, SDP-026, & SDY-022 Common
2x Offerings to the Doomed LON-051 Common
2x Fissure SDJ-028, SDK-032, SDP-028, & SDY-026 Common
2x The Warrior Returning Alive LOD-030 Rare
3x Heart of Clear Water LOD-077 Common
3x Mystical Space Typhoon SDP-032 Common

-Trap Cards- 7
3x Gravity Bind PSV-073 Rare
2x Skull Lair LON-082 Common
2x Magic Jammer SDP-048 Common

Cheap @$$ Deck
MIXING THE STARTER DECKS

By Adam Forristal

The basis of this deck is simple. Use the strongest monsters, Magic and Traps from all four of the starter decks currently on the North American market. If you take a look at all the cards, you'll find several things. Some monsters are great. Others are not.

We'll start with the low level monsters (four and below) that have an attack of at least 1600 or a defense of at least 2000. There's a total of 19 such monsters. It's a few too many for a standard deck, but you can select the ones you want.

There are also many Effect monsters in the decks. They are the orange cards. The great ones have to be handpicked out of the decks. Everyone has their own preferences in Effect monsters. Make sure you select appropriate ones for your deck.

The following Effect monsters will need another card to be the most beneficial to your deck:

Lord of D. (SDK) - You should also include the Flute of Summoning Dragon

Relinquished (SDP) - You should be sure to include the Black Illusion Ritual card.

Toons (SDP) - You must include Toon World.

Now lets consider the high level monsters. There aren't many worth noting. Other than Blue-Eyes White Dragon, the monsters that require two tributes can be ignored entirely. The best of the high level monsters are:

Summoned Skull (SDY)
6/2500/1200

Blue-Eyes White Dragon (SDK)
8/3000/2500

Judge Man (SDK)
6/2200/1500

Blue-Eyes Toon Dragon (SDP)
8/3000/2500

Toon Summoned Skull (SDP)
6/2500/1200

Monsters (20)	Magic (13)
1x Neo the Magic Swordsman (SDY)	1x Dark Hole (All)
2x Giant Soldier of Stone (SDY/SDP)	1x Monster Reborn (All)
1x Battle Ox (SDK)	1x Change of Heart (SDY/SDP/SDJ)
1x La Jinn the Mystical Genie of the Lamp (SDK)	1x Soul Exchange (SDY)
1x 7 Colored Fish (SDJ)	1x Malevolent Nuzzler (SDJ)
1x Darkfire Soldier #1 (SDJ)	1x Giant Trunade (SDJ)
1x Island Turtle (SDJ)	1x Eternal Rest (SDJ)
1x Harpie's Brother (SDJ)	1x Scapegoat (SDJ)
1x Gearfried the Iron Knight (SDJ)	1x Black Pendant (SDP)
1x Summoned Skull (SDY)	1x Mystical Space Typhoon (SDP)
1x Judge Man (SDK)	1x Graceful Charity (SDP)
1x Blue-Eyes White Dragon (SDK)	2x Fissure (All)

Traps (9)

2x Man-Eater Bug (SDY/SDP)	2x Trap Hole (All)
1x Wall of Illusion (SDY)	1x Ultimate Offering (All)
1x Magician of Faith (SDJ)	2x Waboku (SDY/SDJ/SDP)
1x Penguin Soldier (SDJ)	1x Dragon Capture Jar (SDY)
1x Witch of the Black Forest (SDP)	1x Seven Tools of the Bandit (SDJ/SDP)
1x Muka Muka (SDP)	1x Magic Jammer (SDP)
	1x Enchanted Javelin (SDP)

Grand Total: 42 Cards

They aren't really any worth noting in the Joey deck. Also, remember that you can't play the Toons without Toon World on the field.

Magic and Trap cards are a matter of personal preference. Note that Counter-Traps are the fastest cards in the game (spell speed), and the strongest Magic and Traps have been restricted.

I've selected what I consider to be the best of the cards from the four decks and put them all together into one.

It's not a bad deck. I can definitely see it winning some duels. I don't think that its tournament worthy yet, but it's a great start. For anyone who has bought the four starters (or intends to) this is a fairly solid deck.

I'd suggest using it in a few duels (or making your own deck out of the 19 mentioned low level monsters, five tribute monsters and your personal preference/what you think is strongest in Magic, Traps and Effect monsters.) See what happens, at least until you buy a few boosters and make it better.

One last thing, if you want to make Side deck, make it out of the cards from the lists at the top that you didn't include in the deck. All of the cards are beneficial in some way, and you don't know what you might need. ∎

Cheap @$$ Deck
BURN

By_Evan Vargas, a.k.a. SandTrap

Have no money? Need a cheap deck that you can play decently? Zook no further! We have a Cheap @$$ Burn deck just for you.

The main theme is direct damage while hiding under the protection of Magics and Traps. Use the Rabbits, the Jinzos, and the Flowers to cheaply deplete your opponent's LPs (Life Points). While you peck at the opponent's LPs, he or she can't fight back because Gravity Bind will stop almost every monster being played. You can keep pecking away and your opponent will die a horribly slow and embarrassing defeat.

As an added bonus to cheaply attacking your opponent in such a sad, sad way, you can use Dream Clown to destroy his or her monsters and clear a path for more cheapness via White Magical Hat. Not only do you get to cheaply attack with super weak monsters, but you will disrupt your opponent's hand as well. Witch and Sangan are used to easily search for these cheap monsters.

Magic cards

Because this deck is full of weak ATK value monsters, we need Fissure to take out the more powerful con-
tenders, such as your average Beatdown monster like Kycoo the Ghost Destroyer and Gemini Elf. Swords of Revealing Light will also hel keep your monsters protected, and allow you to continue pecking away a your opponent's LPs.

Dark Hole, Monster Reborn, Change of Heart, and Pot of Greed are staples that should be in every deck. The Mystical Space Typhoon makes sure that there won't be any nasty magic c trap cards that get in your way. It wil take care of your opponent's Imperial Orders, Calls of the Haunted, etc. Plu if you play another duelist using Gravity Bind like this deck, you can take care of his or her support and tak the advantage.

Tremendous Fire is a nice Burn card that helps bring down your opponent even faster. You take 500 LP damage, but it's not much of a loss.

Trap cards

Trap cards tend to be played in lower numbers thanks to Magic/Trap removal and Jinzo. However, not in this deck, no sir! This deck uses three Gravity Binds so your monsters stay alive longer to cause more mayhem. The three Trap Holes also help protect the weak monsters by destroying your opponent's monsters before they have a chance to cause any damage.

Waboku is used for more protection and, as a plus, it can chain to enemy magic/trap removal. This is always a nice thing. The Magic Jammers are necessary in order to give support cards like Gravity Bind their own support. The plan is to have Gravity Bind last longer to support the monsters. Confused? You should be! Basically Magic Jammer makes Gravity Bind las

GRAVITY BIND

[TRAP CARD]

PSV-073

1ST Edition

All monsters of Level 4 or higher cannot attack. Their positions may still be changed.

©1996 KAZUKI TAKAHASHI

85742772

longer.

Gravity Bind makes your monsters last nger. If your monsters last longer, en they are much more effective and n deplete more LPs.

Ominous Fortunetelling is an interesting common card. It allows you to ek at your opponent's hand, which a good thing. It also ows you do inflict 700 LP mage if you correctly less the type of card you ve selected, either a onster, Magic, or Trap. ain, another very nice ing.

Most of the time, duelists nd to have more Magics an Monsters or Traps, so ur best bet is to choose agic as the card type to lict the 700 LPs. Plus, by eing which cards your pponent has, you can help epare yourself for whatev-your opponent has anned for you.

For example, if, via minous Fortunetelling, you ow your opponent has a igeki in his hand, it would t be a good idea to keep unch of monsters out on e field for your opponent destroy. By being aware this information, when ur opponent does play

Raigeki, he or she won't kill as many monsters Now you know the secrets of this deck.

However, there is also something else to be aware of when using this deck or a deck that depends on cards like Gravity Bind and Messenger of Peace. In the current environment, there is a lot of magic/trap removal. Many duelists use three Mystical Space Typhoons, one Heavy Storm, and one Harpie's Feather Duster.

If a deck depends on continuous stall

Monsters –15–
[3] Inaba White Rabbit
(LOD-065)
[3] Jinzo #7
(MRD-035)
[3] Rainbow Flower
(MRD-042)
[2] Dream Clown
(MRD-080)
[2] White Magical Hat
(SDJ-021)
[1] Witch of the Black Forest
(SDP-014)
[1] Sangan
(SDJ-019)

Magic –13–
[1] Dark Hole
(SDP-026)
[1] Monster Reborn
(SDJ-035)
[1] Change of Heart
(SDP-030)
[1] Pot of Greed
(TP3-014)
[3] Mystical Space Typhoon
(SDP-032)
[3] Tremendous Fire
(MRD-088)
[3] Fissure
(SDJ-028)

Traps –12–
[3] Gravity Bind
(PSV-073)
[3] Trap Hole
(SDJ-043)
[2] Ominous Fortunetelling
(LOD-094)
[2] Magic Jammer
(SDP-048)
[2] Waboku
(SDY-040)

–40– Cards Total

cards, with such a high level of m/t removal, it is doubtful you can win. Of course, that is why you have the Magic Jammers to help counter this vital point. As long as you have adequate protection and are able to keep your stall cards up and running, you have the opportunity to be victorious.

I don't see this deck as a future winner in tournaments anytime soon. But if you are low on cash and need a crazy deck, this is the way to go. ■

21 Staples
in the Yu-Gi-Oh! game

By_Evan Vargas, a.K.a. The Sand Trap

Hey, we've all been to tournaments, right? We all are trying to see how each duelist ranks against the competition, which deck strategy is better than another: basically, who is better than who. And, of course, we're having some fun as well.

If you take a look at the different tournament-level decks being played right now, you may notice a trend. Many decks use the same cards. These cards are often played in almost every single competitive deck, because they tend to be very good and playable. We deem these cards "Staples".

Staples are cards that work very well in every deck. When you are deciding which cards to put into your new deck, these cards always have priority. If you want to have the best chance to win as many duels and matches as possible, the majority of the staples must be in your deck.

So, ask yourself, "Which cards are considered staples?" Well, let's take a look.

1.) Raigeki (LOB-053)

Raigeki is one of the best Magic cards in the whole Yu-Gi-Oh game. The power to destroy all of your opponent's monsters with a single card is simply incredible. It clears any threat and allows you to go on the offensive. Or, it can be used to destroy a Flip Effect monster so that its Effect does not activate.

Raigeki also can be used to help you survive the next turn, or simply get more card advantage. It gives you "card advantage" by using one of your cards to get rid of a few of your opponent's cards. In this game, card advantage is a necessity to victory.

2.) Dark Hole (LOB-052)

This card is what some call, "Raigeki's little brother." The name certainly fits. With the ability to destroy all monsters on the field, a well-timed Dark Hole can act just like a Raigeki. Use Dark Hole when you don't have a monster on the field. If your opponent has a monster or monsters that can do some serious damage next turn, use Dark Hole.

Even if you do have a monster or two on the field, as long as you can get rid of the threat while not hurting yourself too badly, you will be OK. You could also use Dark Hole to help search through your deck via Sangan or Witch of the Black Forest. You can kill some of your opponent's mon ters along with your Sangan/Witch, then search for a monster that will help you damage or defeat your opponent with an open field, such as Jinzo or Yata-Garasu.

Remember to try to maintain card advantage whenever you can. The more cards you have, the better.

3.) Pot of Greed (LOB-119)

Say hello to the best card in all of Yu-Gi-Oh, Pot of Greed. I wish I could run three. As I've said, having card advantage in Yu-Gi-Oh is a very important aspect of the game. Pot of Greed is a necessity. This card has no downside at all. Play one card to get two, thus giving you a card advantage of +1. It allows you to speed through your deck to grab cards you need in certain situations, or allows you to draw the Monster card that can finish your opponent off, etc.

In a game where draw power is limited, you better be running Pot of Greed or you can expect to lose some duels. If your deck is faster, you can get to your better cards quickly and get an advantage over your opponent. The more cards you have available, the more options you have to cope with the current situation.

Having versatility can seriously make or break a duel. So, to try to be as versatile as possible, you want both speed and card advantage. Pot of Greed is card advantage in its purest form.

4.) Change of Heart (MRD-060)

Change of Heart is another great card that belongs in every deck Out of the six staples, I find it to be the weakest of them all. Nonetheless, it can be useful. It's Jinzo's best friend. You Change of Heart your opponent's monster, and sacrifice it to bring out Dr. J. It's one of the best ways to bring out a Tribute monster.

It is also useful for making an opening in your opponent's Monster field

for a direct attack on his or her LPs (Life Points). Also use it to grab a Flip Effect monster like Magician of Faith. You flip the monster, use the Effect, then tribute it for your big monster, like Jinzo. If a pesky Cyber Jar is blocking your four monster attack, use CoH to take out your opponent before Cyber Jar returns back to him or her.

Th reason why I like this card the least out of the six staples is it goes back to the opponent's side of the field at the end of your turn. If you play CoH and attack with the monster you grabbed then end your turn, you came out with a -1 in card advantage. This is not a good result. You may have done some nice damage, but you don't know what your opponent will do. When your opponent has more options than you do, your little hit may not amount to anything. Always be on guard when using Change of Heart.

5.) Monster Reborn (LOB-118)

Ah, good ol' Monster Reborn. This is one of my favorite cards. The reason? I use Painful Choice to get Jinzo into the graveyard, making it much easier to revive with cards such as this one. Monster Reborn is one of the three main Recursion cards. In Yu-Gi-Oh, where duelists normally summon only one monster per turn, having the ability to summon multiple monsters can be a very beneficial and effective tactic.

You can reborn a powerful Monster, normal summon another monster, and take out your opponent's defenses, all while doing some hefty LP damage. Another great use for Recursion cards such as Monster Reborn is to grab monsters like Sangan and Witch of the Black Forest. You can be sure that you'll be able to search your deck for a Monster card and thus give you a bigger hand.

Also, you can use this same method to tribute that Witch or Sangan for a Tribute monster like Jinzo. It helps to bring the big monster out while searching your deck for another Monster card to help you out. I love this card...*SandTrap snuggles his holo Monster Reborn*...um...yeah, so anyways...

6.) Harpie's Feather Duster (SDD-003)

The Raigeki of Magic and Trap cards. Like its...cousin (or nephew...or something)...HFD is a very powerful card. "M/T" (magic and trap) cards like Premature Burial, Snatch Steal, Mirror Force, etc., need to stay on the field in order to benefit from their Effects.

With HFD, you can clear away the nasty M/T cards. This will make sure you have a clear path against your opponent's monsters, as well as his or her LPs. It allows you to take away your opponent's support and leave them helpless against your superior monsters. What more is there to say? This card is great.

7.) Witch of the Black Forest (MRD-116)

This is one of the best Monsters in the entire game. Witch of the Black Forest is incredible and useful; I don't think any deck can survive without it. I mean, it's so, so good. In most decks, the Witch can search for practically any monster being played. Whenever it dies and goes to the graveyard, you are given the opportunity to adapt to whatever situation you are in, and allows you to find the monster to help you in that situation.

For example, if my opponent just used a Jinzo to kill my Witch, I'll search for Bazoo to take out Jinzo. Or, if my opponent has a GAF in DEF mode and another monster, I'll search for Exiled Force. The next turn I'll use Exiled Force to attack and destroy the GAF, then use its Effect to destroy the other monster. Maximizing your cards to their fullest, is what the Witch is all about. One piece of advice, try to summon the Witch in ATK mode. This way a pesky Nobleman of Crossout won't stop you from searching your deck. Of course, next set Don Zaruug may change that idea, but who knows...

8.) Sangan (MRD-069)

Heh, the Witch's brother, Sangan, is also a very good monster to speed through your deck. Many decks use Witch, Sinister Serpent, Exiled Force, Yata-Garasu, Fiber Jar, etc. Use Sangan to search your deck for a needed card, like grabbing Yata when preparing to lock your opponent. Like the Witch of the Black Forest, card advantage and versatility are good things that this card will provide.

9.) Sinister Serpent (SDD-002)

The little snake can cause some big trouble for your opponent. It can single-handedly (or...wingedly...I don't know...) stop a Yata lock. Currently, Yata is a very dangerous monster that can easily end a duel. Sinister has saved me countless times, and it may well be my favorite Monster. You can also use it to stall by using Sinister Serpent as a wall, or use it in combination with Graceful Charity to make them act like Super Pot of Greeds.

In fact, what I like to do is play Painful Choice and pick five cards including Sinister Serpent and Jinzo. My opponent will most likely choose my Sinister Serpent to go to my hand. With Sinister Serpent in my hand, I play Graceful Charity. Painful Choice + Sinister Serpent + Graceful Charity = 'The Ultimate Combo'. I love it.

10.) Yata-Garasu

Possibly the best Monster card in the game. Although other players may say that Yata needs too much to be effective. Yata can win games on its own, something no other monster can say (well, besides Exodia...but that's different...). All you do is clear the monsters away, clear the M/T away, and attack with Yata. If your opponent doesn't have a Trap card, like Torrential Tribute or Mirror Force, that can stop Yata, or a monster to put in the way, the game is done.

It is sad when your opponent loses with his hand consisting of Raigeki, Snatch Steal, and Jinzo. Luckily, Sinister Serpent can be a serious problem for Yata. Plus, cards like Delinquent Duo and Confiscation can stop Yata in its tracks. Although Yata is a really great monster, there are ways to stop it.

1.) Jinzo (PSV-000)

Well, well, well, if it isn't Jinzo, the monster who changed the way the game is played. Dr. J made playing too many trap cards suicide. As a one tribute, 2400 ATK monster, he's not half bad in battle. Plus, being searchable via Witch of the Black Forest is another huge plus. This is a staple monster for a long, long time. Jinzo's just a bad ass.

2.) Fiber Jar (LOD-056)

Do you need a quick recovery after burning out your hand? Are you facing an army of monsters and only have a Kuriboh to protect you? Look no further because Fiber Jar is the card for you. You get a nice reset and another chance to turn a bad situation into a new one. It works great when you get some shitty hands. However, be careful when flipping it...

13.) Graceful Charity

In this game, draw power is vital. The more draw power you have, the more speed and versatility you have. The deck will run better overall. This card is great speed, even more than Pot of Greed. Pot of Greed is great for speed and card advantage, but Graceful Charity is speed in its truest form. Being able to draw three cards into your deck, plus searching for just the right card, is a truly amazing Effect. Yes, you do have to discard two cards, but in the end you break even in terms of card advantage. If you use Sinister Serpent, you may even gain a slight but significant advantage over your opponent.

14.) Hand Disruption (Delinquent Duo, The Forceful Sentry, and Confiscation)

I grouped the three of these together because they serve the same functions. You can disrupt your opponent's hand, choose which cards you can't deal with easily, and leave him or her at a disadvantage. With Delinquent Duo, you lose one card and your opponent loses two, thus giving you card advantage.

With the other two, you can see what your opponent has planned. You can take away your opponent's disruption or speed, and leave him or her helpless for what you have in your hand. These cards allow you to "ambush" your opponent, and predict what they will play. This allows you to set and move accordingly. Knowing what the opponent has set is a good thing. Plus, with Hand Disruption, the Yata lock can be pulled off much easier. 1000 LPs is nothing compared to the advantages you gain by using these cards.

15.) Heavy Storm

The Dark Hole of M/Ts. The original M/T King. This card, along with HFD and other M/T removal, has made it dangerous to have a few M/Ts set on the field. Without adequate protection via Imperial Order, not many cards can stand the force of this storm (haha, I did that on accident. Heavy Storm...storm...get it? Like, force of this storm...and its Heavy Storm...bah, I give up). Yeah... make sure to have this card waiting for your opponent to set a couple M/Ts down so you can nail them with Heavy Storm and get a two-for-one deal.

16.) Mystical Space Typhoon

This card is awesome. I believe that every deck should be running at least 3 MST (and coincidentally, the max as well). Being able to knock out cards like Premature Burial, Snatch Steal, Imperial Order, Mirror Force, etc. is a powerful tool. The Effect alone makes MST a nice card, but it has another bonus to abuse. It is a Quick-Play Magic card, meaning I can chain it to IO, other M/T removal, Snatch, and other nasty cards or my opponent's turn, stopping any future plans right in their tracks.

17.) Snatch Steal

Snatch Steal is a great way to summon one or two-tribute monsters. Jinzo loves Snatch Steal almost as much as Change of Heart (CoH can't be MST'ed like Snatch Steal can). Plus, being able to swarm your opponent can net you some big damage and field control. If you can attack with more monsters than you opponent can handle, then...well, you win.

18.) Premature Burial

Special Summoning any monster in your graveyard for only 800 LPs is a pretty decent deal. Get back that Exiled Force or Jinzo and wreak havoc all over again. Swarming is good, and this card is for swarming Thus, this card is good. Remember to get back those Witches and Sangans for searching and speed!

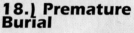

9.) Mirror Force

The Force of the Mirror incredible. Stopping an opponent's attack while destroying the attackers rather nice. Too bad Jinzo makes Mirror Force, along with other Traps, totally useless. Nonetheless, Mirror Force is a very scary card. I remember when I flipped Cyber Jar, got five monsters in ATK mode, and proceeded to slam into a Mirror Force...*shudders*. A very powerful card to watch out for on the scene.

20.) Call of the Haunted

The Trap version of Premature Burial. CotH is one of the best Trap cards I've ever used. Being able to chain to M/T removal to bring Jinzo back from the graveyard is a nice touch. Also, being able to swarm your opponent is always a nice thing, and furthermore, it can make it easy to tribute the big Monsters. Flipping CotH during the Battle Phase to get that last Monster onto the field to attack for the game...ah, CotH is nice.

21.) Imperial Order

Last, but absolutely not least. This card makes playing three MSTs almost a necessity. With so many Magic cards being played (usually around half a duelist's deck), IO can cause some serious problems. With your opponent unable to use Magic cards, you can use your Monsters and Traps to gain the upper hand for a measly 700 LPs per Standby Phase. When you need to use some of your own Magic cards, or if you are tired of paying 700 a turn, just discard it and continue the assault. The best Trap card in the game, in my opinion.

What does this all mean, you ask? Over half of a tournament-level deck are staple cards. Some might say that I didn't put cards on the list that should be considered staples. Others may say that some cards on the list should not be considered staples. Whether or not you agree with the list, you must admit that in order to have the best chance at winning, you should play with the better cards.

Of course, having fun while playing is also important, but winning tends to get you more prizes and trophies. My point? Have fun while winning, or else try to have fun losing. I prefer the first choice, but that's just me.

Thanks for reading.
Evan Vargas, a.k.a. TheSandTrap ∎

How to build

an effective side deck

By Vijay Seixas, a.k.a. SomeGuy

The Side Deck is one aspect in the Yu-Gi-Oh! CCG that I don't see abused as much as it should be. Adopted from the Mother of all Trading and Collectable Card Games (Magic: The Gathering), the Side Deck is similar to the Sideboard in that it consists of 15 cards that are used in between games. Although the main difference is that most Magic players put as much playtesting into their Sideboard as they do to their Main Deck.

From what I've seen, whether it is on the Internet or the local tournament scene, the majority of Yu-Gi-Oh! players put little or no thinking into their Side Deck. The result is they hold many cards that will never see any play.

Of course, there are some legitimate reasons for this approach. One of them is that the Yu-Gi-Oh! CCG is unbalanced by the fact that tournament-winning decks are in small variety. Another reason is that a large number of Yu-Gi-Oh! players consist of small children, who usually lack the experience to correctly make an effective Side Deck, or even Main Deck for that matter.

If you know how to build a solid Side Deck, great; if you don't, here's your chance. In this article I will go through all the steps in creating the perfect counter Side Deck for your local metagame or tournament scene. Keep in mind that a well-built Side Deck will support your deck in winning more games.

Step One:

The first step in creating an effective Side Deck is analyzing what your main competition at your local tournaments play. There are a few ways to do this. If you're good friends with the fellow players then you should know what type of deck they run. If you don't know them, you can wait until you face them. Or, if you finish one of your tournament matches, you can quickly scout around the tournament area.

In between rounds and/or before or after the tournament, be sure to do some note taking as to what is being played by the top players. This will help

SINISTER SERPENT

[REPTILE/EFFECT]
During your Standby Phase, if a "Sinister Serpent" exists in your Graveyard, you can return the "Sinister Serpent" to your hand.

ATK/ 300 DEF/ 250
©1996 KAZUKI TAKAHASHI

HEART OF CLEAR WATER

[MAGIC CARD]

BUBBLE CRASH

[TRAP CARD]

The Legendary Fisherman/Water based Decks: Dust Tornado, Kycoo the Ghost Destroyer, Possessed Dark Soul

keep you be more organized when you begin building your Side Deck. Also, keep in mind that some of your main competition may use a different deck during the next tournament. This is why a regular analysis for several weeks is necessary.

Step Two:

Once you've gathered the essential data, you can begin researching how many cards you should dedicate to counter a specific deck. Let's say you recorded two well-built Exodia decks being played on your local tournament scene. Most tournaments average 32 players.

Unless the Exodia players are the two toughest opponents there, you shouldn't dedicate more than 3 or 4 cards in your Side Deck to this type of deck. The odds are that you will not face them every single week.

Another factor you should consider is whether your deck is vulnerable to another specific deck(s) or card(s). If so, you need to include a fair amount of counter strategies in your Side Deck. To help, I will list the basic Side Deck options to some of the most popular

decks around. If you see something obvious that is not on the list (i.e., Exodia: no Confiscation; Clown Control: no Mystical Space Typhoon), it's because these cards should already be included in your Main Deck.

Exodia: Card Destruction, Kycoo the Ghost-Destroyer, Exchange, Morphing Jar, Soul Release

Clown Control: Possessed Dark Soul, Dust Tornado, Skull Lair

Suicide Beatdown: Scapegoat, Waboku

Warrior-type Decks: Array of Revealing Light, Spear Dragon, Scapegoat

Fiend-type Decks: Array of Revealing Light, Exile of the Wicked

Fire Princess/Life Gain Decks: Bad Reaction to Simochi, Prohibition

The Last Warrior From Another Planet/Thousand Eyes Restrict based Decks: Bottomless Trap Hole, Torrential Tribute, Jowgen the Spiritualist, Kycoo the Ghost Destroyer

Direct Damage/Burn Decks: Dust Tornado, Nobleman of Crossout, Ceasefire, Magic Drain, Dark Ruler Ha Des

Step Three:

The final step is simply perfection. From here on, all you need to do is playtest and tweak. You find out which cards are helping you, and which are just taking up space. It's rare to find a metagame that does not constantly change, so you always need to stay on your toes. This means adding and dropping cards as you see fit, especially once a new set has been released.

The end result should give you plenty of knowledge on the subject of Side Decking. Trust me, a properly built counter Side Deck will give you a noticeable advantage in the long run.

All right, we've taken a look at the basic counter version of the Side Deck that most top tournament players love to abuse. Now I'll discuss a whole new outlook at Side Decking. This new option allows you to mess with your opponent's head by giving him or her a nice surprise. Although it may not be as effective, it's definitely a lot more fun.

The whole idea revolves around using the entire 15 cards in your Side Deck to their maximum potential. When you're running a 40 card deck, you can change the entire strategy of your deck when Side Decking. I've listed a couple decks that can benefit from swapping strategies using their Side Deck.

Clown Control

(For more on the Clown Control deck, check out my other article in the book)

Monster Cards: 15

3x Dream Clown
2x White Magical Hat
2x Marauding Captain
1x Witch of the Black Forest
1x Sangan
1x Jinzo
1x Sinister Serpent
1x Yata-Garasu
1x Injection Fairy Lily
1x Fiber Jar
1x Exiled Force

Magic Cards: 19

3x Mystical Space Typhoon
2x Graceful Charity
2x Heart of Clear Water
1x The Warrior Returning Alive
1x Reinforcement of the Army
1x Monster Reborn
1x Pot of Greed
1x Change of Heart
1x Raigeki
1x Dark Hole

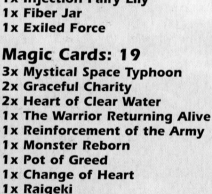

1x Harpie's Feather Duster
1x Delinquent Duo
1x Confiscation
1x The Forceful Sentry
1x Premature Burial

Trap Cards: 6

3x Gravity Bind
1x Imperial Order
1x Mirror Force
1x Magic Cylinder

Side Deck: 15

3x Goblin Attack Force
2x Spear Dragon
2x Gemini Elf
1x Bazoo the Soul-Eater
1x Snatch Steal
2x Torrential Tribute
1x Call of the Haunted
1x Reinforcement of the Army
1x Painful Choice
1x Nobleman of Crossout

As you can see with this type of Side Deck, Clown Control can easily turn into either Warrior Beatdown or New Age Beatdown. Either way, you can catch your opponent off guard during the next game. It's excellent strategizing for you, and is used when he or she has possibly Side Decked useless against your original Clown Control.

The next Deck and Side Deck is more for casual play, but it can be a beast if played correctly. However, it does rely on getting good draws.

Exodia Control

Monster Cards: 15

1x Exodia the Forbidden One
1x Left Arm of the Forbidden One
1x Right Arm of the Forbidden One
1x Left Leg of the Forbidden One
1x Right Leg of the Forbidden One
2x Penguin Soldier
2x Magician of Faith
2x Mask of Darkness
1x Witch of the Black Forest
1x Sangan
1x Sinister Serpent
1x Fiber Jar

Magic Cards: 14

3x Scapegoat
2x Graceful Charity
2x Messenger of Peace
1x Dark Hole
1x Monster Reborn
1x Premature Burial
1x Pot of Greed
1x Card Destruction
1x Upstart Goblin
1x Painful Choice

Trap Cards: 11

3x Waboku
2x A Feint Plan
2x Backup Soldier

2x **Gravity Bind**
x **Call of the Haunted**
x **Imperial Order**

Side Deck: 15
3x **Jowgen the Spiritualist**
1x **Injection Angel Lily**
1x **Exiled Force**
3x **Inspection**
1x **Raigeki**
1x **Harpie's Feather Duster**
3x **Solemn Judgment**
2x **Last Turn**

If you get some decent draws, it will be difficult for an unsuspecting opponent to beat an Exodia deck with this much stall. During the second game, your opponent will be more prepared mentally and physically. He or she will likely Side Deck heavily against your Exodia deck.

Oops. They won't expect a deck based around the instant win combo of Last Turn and Jowgen the Spiritualist. Yu-Gi-Oh! doesn't get anymore entertaining that this.

As you can see, the Side Deck is a remarkable but often overlooked part of this Collectable Card Game. There are many interesting aspects and combinations that, when mastered, can be game breaking. ∎

Dungeon Dice Monsters

Game Boy Advance

Pojo's Review

Let's just preface this whole review by saying, if you liked the episode where Yugi battled Duke Devlin while playing Dungeon Dice Monsters (DDM), then you'll probably like this game.

I'm not going to explain how DDM is played in this review. Duke Devlin did a much better job explaining how to play this game during the Anime than I'd ever do. I actually thought it was amazing how good of a teacher the Duker actually is! I'm just going to tell you my thoughts on the game.

First off, the game is extremely faithful to the episodes in which YuGi & Duke battled. You select dice. You roll dice. You summon monsters. You dimension your monsters. You move. You attack. You block. Basically everything you saw in the show happens in the game.

Some of the things I found interesting in the game play that weren't noted on the show. Some monsters have flying, and can fly over enemies on their path. This uses more "movement crests" than a usual move, but can be helpful. And in the same fashion, some monsters have a digging ability that lets them tunnel under monsters.

Also, there is one more way to win besides attacking your opponents "3 hearts". If you summon all 5 pieces of Exodia, you automatically win.

Game play on the Game Boy is pretty straightforward. This game is easier to learn than Duel Monsters. I'd keep the instruction booklet handy the first couple of times you play a match. As it can be confusing to understand the controls, but once you do, the game is very simple to play.

If any of your monsters have special abilities (i.e.: increase attack power, or defense), you will be prompt-

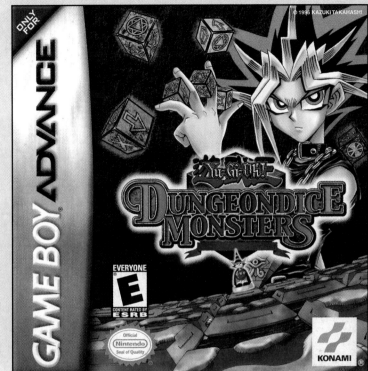

Rex Raptor

As the name suggests, he has an army of dinosaurs under his command.

...ed as to whether you want to use ...hese abilities prior to attacking, or get...ing attacked. Pretty nice.

You start off with slightly more than ...he 15 dice you need to play the ...game. You earn money to buy more ...dice as you duel. You can buy & sell ...dice in Grandpa's shop. Of course I

Petit-Dragon

don't think Grandpa has a dice store in the show? Duke does! But everything can't be perfect. ;-)

Sound & Graphics are about what you expect for the GBA. When monsters attack, an animation will show your dragon (or whatever monster you are attacking with) attacking the defender. What's nice is that Konami gives you the ability to shut off this redundant animation if you are sick of seeing it.

Like I said above, if you liked the episode where Yugi battled Duke Devlin while playing DDM, then you'll probably like this game. If you thought the game was stupid compared to Duel Monsters, stick with the electronic CCG versions.

I kind of wish the game had more of an RPG feel to it. It would be cool if you could be wandering around a city with your little dude and finding people to duel, like in Pokemon. Walk down an alley, and have Rex Raptor

Kuriboh

waiting to challenge you? Get challenged by a scantily clad Mai Valentine! Yeah ... that would be more like it! ;-)

There is essentially no storyline whatsoever, which I find somewhat disappointing. You just jump right into tournaments.

I still give this game a "Thumbs Up" though.

If you want to know more on DDM, visit the www.pojo.com website. There's also a Forum on our Popular Message Boards for discussing Dungeon Dice Monsters as well. ∎

Be Your Own Hotshot Duelist III:

Yu-Gi-Oh! Worldwide Edition

By Nick Moore, a.k.a. NickWhiz1

Since Konami is always in pursuit of the almighty dollar (and aren't we all?), they have redone the Japanese Duel Monsters 6 and released it worldwide. The game itself can handle 6 different languages (basically, English plus the English equivalent of Japanese, German, Spanish, Italian, and French). How is the game? Let's find out:

Review
Play Control:

The play control is the same as Eternal Duelist Soul (EDS). This time there's only a 68 page instruction manual. Guess they used a smaller font =/

Graphics:

For a Game Boy Advance, the graphics are OK. The cards have accurate pictures, albeit a little more digitized. Otherwise, it's pretty plain.

Sound:

The sound is nothing to get excited about, really. Some of the duel themes are pretty catchy, but there's little in the way of sound effects. There are no voiceovers, which I'm sure the GBA can handle (at least, I think so =/) (cut & paste from EDS)

Plot:

This game is a little more involved in the YGO universe. You are thrown into the Battle City tournament and must wander around to find random opponents. OK, you don't actually walk around as in Zelda walk-around, you're just shown a map with 14 areas and you "walk" between areas.

Difficulty:

This game is more difficult than EDS because almost all of the opponents are strong. You will be facing random opponents from the beginning until you identify them all. Thus, you'll need to be strong from the beginning.

Game Play:

The game play here is VERY solid, playing almost exactly like the Yu-Gi-Oh! Trading Card Game released by Konami/Upper Deck. The few differences in the game (Toon World and Morphing Jar #2 come to mind) are because the texts/rulings for those cards were different in Japan than what they are now.

Overall:

 (83%)

This game is even better than EDS. I should give it 5 bonus chips because I've got good promos with the game (two of which are practically staples).

Strategies

Each of the starter decks has enough cards to get you started on the right track, with some decently powered monsters and some powerful Magic/Traps.

If you see an opponent's screen that is fuzzy, that means that you have not faced them yet, meaning you must challenge them blind and hope you have the cards to beat them.

Pick a theme. Beatdown is probably the best theme to pick, although you are free to use Exodia, Burner, or anything you want. (I've grown fond of a Deck Destruction deck myself.)

If you're going to lose, you can just turn the game off before the game ends and you won't have a loss counted against you ^_^

The God Cards AREN'T in this game. Sorry =(

Restrictions:

One Per Deck – Bell of Destruction, Call of the Haunted, Card Destruction, Ceasefire, Change of Heart, Confiscation, Cyber Jar, Dark Hole, Delinquent Duo, Exodia the Forbidden One, Harpie's Feather Duster, Heavy Storm, Imperial Order, Jinzo, Left Arm of the Forbidden One, Left Leg of the Forbidden One, Limiter Removal, Mage Power, Magic Cylinder, Mirror Force, Monster Reborn, Morphing Jar, Painful Choice, Pot of Greed, Premature Burial, Raigeki, Right Arm of the Forbidden One, Right Leg of the Forbidden One, Slate Warrior, Snatch Steal, Swords of Revealing Light, The Forceful Sentry, United We Stand, Upstart Goblin, Witch of the Black Forest

Two Per Deck – Backup Soldier, Graceful Charity, Morphing Jar #2, Nobleman of Crossout, Sangan

I know this will come up, so I'll say it now. Bazoo, Kycoo, and Skull Lair follow the Japanese rulings (you can only remove monsters). Live with it =/

This battle... All will depend on how much of your spirit goes into the deck! Every tactic should be weighed with your heart.

Code	Card
40619825	Axe of Despair
83555666	Bell of Destruction
97077563	Call of the Haunted
72892473	Card Destruction
04031928	Change of Heart
34124316	Cyber Jar
53129443	Dark Hole
44763025	Delinquent Duo
37043180	Dimensional Warrior
69140098	Gemini Elf
79571449	Graceful Charity
18144506	Harpie's Feather Duster
19613556	Heavy Storm
61740673	Imperial Order
77585513	Jinzo
83746708	Mage Power
62279055	Magic Cylinder
77414722	Magic Jammer
31560081	Magician of Faith
07359741	Mechanicalchaser
44095762	Mirror Force
83764718	Monster Reborn
05318639	Mystical Space Typhoon
71044499	Nobleman of Crossout
93920745	Penguin Soldier
55144522	Pot of Greed
70828912	Premature Burial
12580477	Raigeki
26202165	Sangan
03819470	Seven Tools of the Bandit
78636495	Slate Warrior
45986603	Snatch Steal
70781052	Summoned Skull
72302403	Swords of Revealing Light
04206964	Trap Hole
56747793	United We Stand
14898066	Vorse Raider
78010363	Witch of the Black Forest

Passwords

These are a few cards that will help you with the game, and their corresponding passwords. To get any card up to the end of English Labyrinth of Nightmare in this game, use the codes in the lower-left hand corner of your Yu-Gi-Oh! Trading Card Game cards. Remember that you can only use a password once.

Events

Duelist Weekly: Every Monday, win or lose, you'll get a special pack of five cards. If you win on this day, you'll still get your normal pack choice (in addition to your weekly pack).

Saturday Tournament: Every Saturday, one of the 14 spots on the map will host a tournament. It is a one-match duel against any opponent who is currently available in your game. If you win, you will get a special pack of five cards. There is a pattern to the Saturday Tournaments. It starts at the Subway Station (the area in the middle with the giant peninsula, also the place where you begin). It follows in a spiral pattern around Battle City. It will go up one area, right one area, down two areas, left one area, up three areas, up-right one area, right two areas, down two areas, and back left to the starting point.

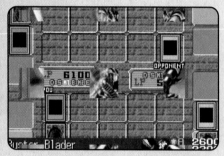

Target Week: Every eighth Sunday, there will be a special event called Target Week. You will be given two opponents, and you will have to find and duel them before the next Monday. If you defeat both of them in time, you will gain access to the rare Millennium Eye Yellow booster, and you will get bonus points.

Challengers Cup: Every 13th Friday, a special three round tournament will be held at one of the areas on the right side of Battle City (it seems to be somewhat random). If you win all three rounds (each match is against an opponent you have access to), you will win a special pack of five cards.

KC Cup: Every 24th Friday, a special three round tournament will be held at the Subway Station (the area in the middle with the giant peninsula, also the place where you begin). If you win all three rounds (each a match against an opponent you have access to), you will win a special pack of five cards.

Ghouls: On the eighth Sunday, and every third Sunday afterwards, there will be an announcement warning about the presence of Ghouls (also known as Rare Hunters) in the city. You will have a random chance of running into one of the five Ghouls. If you defeat one, you get a special pack

of five cards. If you beat all five, you will gain access to the Phantom Pyramid (I'll discuss it a little further down in the article).

Normal Duelists

All of these Duelists are available from the start. You have to hunt them down.

Bakura Ryou - He has a few decent monsters like The Bistro Butcher and La Jinn, but I'd be careful going into this game. He has a variety of Magic and Traps that can really mess you up. He may have Dark Necrofear, but I've never seen him play it, so who knows.

Espa Roba - Just like in the anime, Espa Roba relies mostly on Machines, and mostly weak ones. Just watch out for Jinzo, because I'm sure you all know what he does.

Ishizu Isthar - This can be a pretty hard game. Ishizu uses a full Light deck, with Luminous Spark and plenty of potent Light monsters. She also uses the St. Joan set, and those Forgiving Maidens can really get on your nerves with 2000 Defense. Joan has 3300 attack power while Spark is out, so tread lightly.

Joey Wheeler - Wow, someone pumped up his deck. He uses Warriors and Beast-Warriors, so he has access to some strong cards like Panther Warrior, Zombyra the Dark, and Goblin Attack Force. As with Roba, watch out for Jinzo, because, well, you know =/

Mai Valentine - Once again, Mai is using the Harpie Lady combo, and we all know how annoying that can be. If she manages to swarm her Harpies, be careful because she will run over you in a hurry.

Mako Tsunami - Uses the whole Water combo, blah blah blah, abuses Umi + Tornado Wall, blah blah blah, uses 7 Colored Fish, Giant Red Seasnake, Fortress Whale, and The Legendary Fisherman, blah blah blah.

Rex Raptor - He uses Dinosaurs. What a surprise. Most of his monsters are weak (<1600 ATK) and won't pose a threat.

Seto Kaiba - Probably the toughest opponent in the game. Kaiba has stacked his deck with high attack monsters (Vorse Raider, Slate Warrior, Gemini Elf, and Goblin Attack Force), and uses his signature Blue-Eyes White Dragon, of course. However, he also uses the deadly one turn KO combo with Cyber-Stein. Cyber-Stein will allow him to pay 5000 LP to Special Summon his Blue-Eyes Ultimate Dragon. He then attaches Megamorph to it, increasing its ATK power to 9000. You know where this is going =/

Tea Gardner - A very weak duelist. She has a couple good Female monsters (like Fire Princess), but nothing to worry about.

Trusdale - He got toned down quite a bit from EDS. He still uses Exodia and one Blue-Eyes White Dragon, but he'll rarely gets them out. Other than those few, he uses weak cards.

Weevil Underwood - Gee, I wonder what kind of cards he uses. I wonder. Anyways, finish him off quickly, because some of his insects have nasty effects, like Man-Eater Bug and Needle Worm.

Yami Yugi - I would say he's a little more powerful than in EDS. His deck revolves around Valkyrion the Magna Warrior and Dark Magician. He has some potent cards like the above two and the Magician of Black Chaos. He also uses some monsters like Gemini Elf. His main weakness is his reliance on high-level monsters. If you keep destroying his monsters, he'll be left with nothing to do.

Ghouls

I wonder who these are…=/

Arkana - Uses a deck similar to Yami Yugi from EDS. Of course, his main theme is also the Dark Magician, but he uses other Yugi-esque cards. Not very hard to beat.

Odion - Oh geez, I hate this guy! If you think you've seen a player use a lot of Traps, you haven't seen ANYTHING yet. Odion's deck is almost entirely Traps. The few monsters he uses are pretty good (Vorse Raider, Gate Warrior, Morphing Jar, etc.), and he has some good Magics, but he has a ton of Traps which can block almost any move you make. The key is to get Jinzo out as soon as possible. Once you do that, he's laughable. You must carry Feather Duster, Heavy Storm, 3 MST, and Jinzo for this one.

Rare Hunter - This deck is Exodia in its purest form, and I think he even uses Painful Choice/Backup Soldier! (very rarely, though). Use the standard Exodia-killing strategies on him.

Strings - No Slifer here. Instead, he just wants to deck you out! I suggest carrying Royal Command/Nobleman of Crossout for this game, because he uses plenty of nasty Flip Effect monsters.

Umbra/Lumis - These guys aren't very hard here. They use mostly weak monsters, so they won't be a problem.

Phantom Pyramid

You will unlock this once you have defeated all five Ghouls. To the best of my knowledge, you only get one chance to beat this thing. I'm not sure, though.

Level 1 - Possessed Tea

Whoa, she sure got powerful in a hurry! This deck is straight Fire Princess, and played correctly, Fire Princess is a very dangerous deck. She also uses powerful cards like Needle Worm to take you out in a different way. This is one of the harder duels you'll have in this game.

Level 2 - Odion

He's the same as usual, which is bad news, because he's fairly tough.

Level 3 - Possessed Joey

He seems to be the same, just slightly more powerful. He's still not an easy opponent, though.

Level 4 - Yami Marik

For being the final "boss" in the game, Marik isn't really all that difficult. His deck is similar to Strings, in that he aims to deck you out. This is accomplished with Needle Worm, Morphing Jar, Morphing Jar #2, and Gravekeeper's Servant. Beyond that, he doesn't have a whole lot going for him.

Welcome to Battle City, duelists!!! This city is here for dueling and provides duelists with the opportunity to test their skills!

Unlocked Duelists

These are duelists that you have to perform special actions to unlock.

Kaiba Mokuba - Lose a total of ten duels between all characters.

There's a reason you unlock him if you lose ten times. He's pathetically easy. The strongest monster he uses is Kanan the Swordmistress (1400 ATK), and he almost never uses Magic/Traps. However, every once in a great while he can pull the Cyber-Stein combo. Watch out for it.

All Ghouls - Beat the Phantom Pyramid.

By beating the Pyramid, you unlock all five Ghouls, as well as Marik.

Shadi - Beat the Phantom Pyramid.

Shadi randomly uses another duelist's deck, so it's like choosing a random opponent.

Pegasus - Acquire the Toon World card.

What a surprise, he uses Toon monsters. Of course, the weakness is the Toon World card, so aim for that first. He also has a couple of powerful monsters like Vorse Raider.

Bandit Keith - Get at least five more wins than losses against all opponents

He may act tough, but he's not. He uses all Machines, which is good news because the strongest Level Four Machine is Mechanicalchaser (1850/800). His higher ups are all

Level Seven or higher, requiring two Tributes.

Duke Devlin - Defeat every (and I mean every) other opponent at least once.

For the final duelist you unlock, Devlin is a wimp. He uses weenie swarm cards (Giant Germ, Nimble Momonga, Bubonic Vermin), as well as the Graceful/Skull Dice cards. He's very easy to beat, albeit a little annoying for a little while.

Limit Tournament

Once you beat the Pyramid, you will also unlock the Limit Tournament. This is a series of ten duels where the cards you use are restricted beyond the Restriction List. A win in this tournament will give you the option to turn off the Restriction List.

Game #1

Location: The bottommost area on the right side of the harbor.

Limitation: The only monsters you can use are Warriors and Beast-Warriors.

Game #2

Location: On the leftmost side of Battle City, the second area from the bottom

Limitation: The only monsters you can use are Spellcasters.

Game #3

Location: On the leftmost side of Battle City, the top area.

Limitation: The only monsters you can use are Dragons.

Game #4

Location: On the top row of Battle City, the middle area.

Limitation: The only monsters you can use are Insects.

Game #5

Location: On the rightmost side of Battle City, the middle area.

Limitation: The only monsters you can use are those with levels of four or lower.

Game #6

Location: Across the harbor from Game #1

Limitation: The only monsters you can use are those with less than 1000 ATK.

Game #7

Location: Between Games #2 & #3

Limitation: The only monsters you can use are those with less than 1000 DEF.

Game #8

Location: Next to Game #4

Limitation: The only monsters you can use are Normal Monsters.

Game #9

Location: The area in the upper-right-most corner

Limitation: You can only use Monsters and Trap cards.

Game #10

Location: Below Game #5

Limitation: You can only use Monsters.

The Ten Symbols

Once you beat the Pyramid, you will notice ten symbols on the Options screen. You can light these up by performing the following actions:

- Defeat each opponent in the game at least ten times

- Open each booster pack at least once

- Win at least 50,000 Duel Points

- Win the Saturday Tournament at least once in each area (not necessarily in order, though)

- Win the Challenger's Cup

- Win the KC Cup

- Sometimes when you challenge a duelist, another related duelist in the same area will challenge you instead. Win at least one such duel.

- Get at least one copy of every card in the game. You will get this once you beat the Limit Tournament.

- Win the Limit Tournament.

- Defeat Marik's Phantom Pyramid (you'll instantly have this one)

Unlocking Boosters

Here is a list of all the booster packs and how to unlock them.

Dark Magician - Already unlocked
Mystical Elf - Already unlocked
Red-Eyes Black Dragon - Already unlocked
Harpie Lady - Already unlocked
Gate Guardian Pieces - Already unlocked
Great Moth - Already unlocked
Launcher Spider - Already unlocked
Black Luster Soldier - Already unlocked
Blue-Eyes White Dragon - Acquire a Blue-Eyes White Dragon.
Exodia - Acquire an Exodia the Forbidden One
Black Skull Dragon - Acquire a Red-Eyes Black Dragon.
Barrel Dragon - Acquire a Barrel Dragon.
Relinquished - Keep your Duelist Points at 5000 or higher.
Blue-Eyes Toon Dragon - Keep your Duelist Points at 10,000 or higher.
Buster Blader - Keep your Duelist Points at 20,000 or higher.
The Legendary Fisherman - Keep your Duelist Points at 30,000 or higher.
The Masked Beast - Win the Saturday Tournament, Challenger's Cup, and KC Cup at least once.
FINAL - Defeat all normal (i.e. not unlocked) opponents at least ten times
Blue-Eyes Ultimate Dragon - Win the Saturday tournament at least once
Dark Magician Girl - Win the Saturday tournament at least ten times
Red-Eyes Black Metal Dragon - Keep all of the boosters above unlocked
Graceful Charity - Win at least three games in a row. If you lose a game, you have to win at least three more in a row to reunlock this.
Millennium Puzzle Brown - This will appear on the fifth Sunday, then every fourth Sunday afterwards. It will only

appear on those days.

Millennium Eye Pink - Have at least 500 total cards.
Millennium Eye Green - Have at lea 1000 total cards.
Millennium Puzzle Black - Have at least 70% of the different cards in the game (around 757 different cards)
Millennium Eye Yellow - You only have access to this once you have defeated the second opponent of Target Week. It is the only time you ca open this booster.

Conclusion

Hopefully, my short (yeah right!) walkthrough will help you with this game. I didn't include all the information I could because of space limitations, plus what fun would it be to te you guys everything? Play the game and figure out its secrets _ ■